BIRTHDAYS PAST, BIRTHDAYS PRESENT

by Alan Ayckbourn

SAMUEL FRENCH

Copyright © 2019 by Haydonning Limited
All Rights Reserved

BIRTHDAYS PAST, BIRTHDAYS PRESENT is fully protected under the copyright laws of the British Commonwealth, including Canada, the United States of America, and all other countries of the Copyright Union. All rights, including professional and amateur stage productions, recitation, lecturing, public reading, motion picture, radio broadcasting, television, online/digital production, and the rights of translation into foreign languages are strictly reserved.

ISBN 978-0-573-13256-8

concordtheatricals.co.uk
concordtheatricals.com

FOR AMATEUR PRODUCTION ENQUIRIES

UNITED KINGDOM AND WORLD
EXCLUDING NORTH AMERICA
licensing@concordtheatricals.co.uk
020-7054-7200

Each title is subject to availability from Concord Theatricals, depending upon country of performance.

CAUTION: Professional and amateur producers are hereby warned that *BIRTHDAYS PAST, BIRTHDAYS PRESENT* is subject to a licensing fee. The purchase, renting, lending or use of this book does not constitute a license to perform this title(s), which license must be obtained from the appropriate agent prior to any performance. Performance of this title(s) without a license is a violation of copyright law and may subject the producer and/or presenter of such performances to penalties. Both amateurs and professionals considering a production are strongly advised to apply to the appropriate agent before starting rehearsals, advertising, or booking a theatre. A licensing fee must be paid whether the title is presented for charity or gain and whether or not admission is charged.

This work is published by Samuel French, an imprint of Concord Theatricals. Ltd.

The Professional Rights in this play are controlled by Casarotto Ramsay & Associates Limited, 3rd Floor, 7 Savoy Court, Strand, London WC2R 0EX.

No one shall make any changes in this title for the purpose of production. No part of this book may be reproduced, stored in a retrieval system, scanned, uploaded, or transmitted in any form, by any means, now known or yet to be invented, including mechanical, electronic, digital, photocopying, recording, videotaping, or otherwise, without the prior written permission of the publisher. No one shall share this title, or part of this title, to any social media or file hosting websites.

The moral right of Alan Ayckbourn to be identified as author of this work has been asserted in accordance with Section 77 of the Copyright, Designs and Patents Act 1988.

USE OF COPYRIGHTED MUSIC

A licence issued by Concord Theatricals to perform this play does not include permission to use the incidental music specified in this publication. In the United Kingdom: Where the place of performance is already licensed by the PERFORMING RIGHT SOCIETY (PRS) a return of the music used must be made to them. If the place of performance is not so licensed then application should be made to PRS for Music (www.prsformusic.com.). A separate and additional licence from PHONOGRAPHIC PERFORMANCE LTD.(www. ppluk.com) may be needed whenever commercial recordings are used. Outside the United Kingdom: Please contact the appropriate music licensing authority in your territory for the rights to any incidental music.

USE OF COPYRIGHTED THIRD-PARTY MATERIALS

Licensees are solely responsible for obtaining formal written permission from copyright owners to use copyrighted third-party materials (e.g., artworks, logos) in the performance of this play and are strongly cautioned to do so. If no such permission is obtained by the licensee, then the licensee must use only original materials that the licensee owns and controls. Licensees are solely responsible and liable for clearances of all third-party copyrighted materials, and shall indemnify the copyright owners of the play(s) and their licensing agent, Concord Theatricals Ltd., against any costs, expenses, losses and liabilities arising from the use of such copyrighted third-party materials by licensees.

IMPORTANT BILLING AND CREDIT REQUIREMENTS

If you have obtained performance rights to this title, please refer to your licensing agreement for important billing and credit requirements.

BIRTHDAYS PAST, BIRTHDAYS PRESENT was first produced by the Stephen Joseph Theatre, Scarborough (Round auditorium) on 10th September 2019. The performacne was directed by Alan Ayckbourn, Set Designer Kevin Jenkins, Sound Associate Paul Stear, Lighting by Jason Taylor. The cast was as follows:

MICKY . . . . Russell Dixon
MEG . . . . Jemma Churchill
ADRIAN. . . . . .Jamie Baughan
GRACE/FAITH/CHARITY/HOPE. . . . . Naomi Petersen

CHARACTERS

MICKY – the father
MEG – the mother
ADRIAN – the son

GRACE – Adrian's current girlfriend*
FAITH – Adrian's wife*
CHARITY – a call girl*
HOPE – his sister's friend*

*played by the same actor

SETTING

The time frame of the scenes are meant to show us something about the attitudes and prejudices that often existed during those years.

Scene One:	Micky and Meg's living room, round about now.
Scene Two:	A private room at The Swan Hotel, fifteen years ago.
Scene Three:	Adrian's flat, twenty-five years ago.
Scene Four:	Adrian's room in his parents' house, thirty-eight years ago.

AUTHOR'S NOTES

Birthdays Past, Birthdays Present was written and presented to mark the year of Alan Ayckbourn's own 80th birthday.

Welcome to Ecraf.

Early on, very early on, in my writing career, someone asked me what I was planning to write next.

Being very early on, I was foolish enough to tell them.

Now any experienced writer will warn you that telling anyone what you are planning to write next is a sure way to scupper the project. In this creative business, a germinating seed of an idea prematurely exposed to the cold light of logicality is inevitably doomed to shrivel and die of shock.

So, back in those days, I foolishly told them I was planning to write a farce backwards (working title Ecraf), which would start with four trouser-less clergymen trapped in a cupboard, and then work steadily backwards in time finally to reveal what on earth had caused things to lead to that.

Naturally, the idea never saw the light of day. Now here we are fifty years and eighty plays later and all is forgiven and forgotten.

It is no longer called Ecraf and there's no sign of a clergyman, not even a fully clothed one.

But it does go backwards and there's certainly a cupboard - though you'll have to wait for that.

Starting at the end, hopefully, will prompt you to wonder what on earth caused things to lead to this.

If all goes according to plan, you'll then be intrigued enough to stay with the story through till the very beginning.

Alan Ayckbourn

ACT I

Scene One

(**MICKY**'s eightieth. The front room of **MICKY** and **MEG**'s semi-detached house. Dotted around are several birthday cards. On a side table in one corner, there are various birthday gifts, all still gift wrapped. **MEG**, seventy-five, is busying around preparing the main table for tea. During the next, she struggles to open up the table and extend the gate leg section. **MICKY** watches her from his chair.)

MICKY. Who's coming, then? Who is it we're expecting?

MEG. *(As she fiddles with the table.)* Adrian. And his new girlfriend. He's bringing her as well.

MICKY. Another one, then? *(Watching her.)* Manage that, can you?

MEG. I can manage. I always find it so fiddly. Fiddly thing!

MICKY. Aye, it's always been fiddly. It were fiddly thirty years ago, when we first bought it.

MEG. *(Straightening up.)* There. That'll have to do. It should hold. Providing no one stands on it. Sorry, you'll have to do without your birthday cabaret, this year.

MICKY. That's a shame. Not going to do your fan dance for me, then?

MEG. Chance'd be a fine thing. I'd never get up there, would I? Even if I did, I'd never get down again. Right. I'll fetch things. They'll be here soon. *(As she goes.)* Grace. This one's called Grace, remember?

MICKY. Grace. *(Calling.)* Got to the G's already, has he? He gets through them, doesn't he? Collects women like I collected cigarette cards. Hope this one works out better than the last few.

> (**MEG** *returns with a tablecloth which she proceeds to spread over the table.*)

MEG. *(Returning.)* Well, he's still searching, isn't he? Ever since Faith left he's been looking for someone to take her place. It's not easy, not when you're his age. Fingers crossed this Grace will be the right one for him. She sounded nice on the phone. Gentle and soft-spoken, you know.

MICKY. Tenth time lucky, eh?

MEG. I hope we haven't seen the last of Faith, though. I know they're divorced but I hope we can keep in touch. I really grew fond of her, you know. Over the years.

MICKY. I found her a right misery.

> (**MEG** *goes off again.*)

MEG. Yes, I know you did. Made no secret of it either, did you? *(As she goes.)* She had good reason to be miserable, poor lass. What with all her problems. Her health problems. And then, of course, she had her mental problems as well, on top of all that...

MICKY. *(Calling.)* She was, she was bloody mental full stop, if you ask me. Adrian was a saint putting up with it as long as he did –

> (**MEG** *returns with two plates of clingfilm covered sandwiches.*)

MEG. *(As she enters.)* Well, that's his nature, isn't it?

MICKY. I wouldn't have put up with it –

MEG. I know you wouldn't –

MICKY. I'd have been off like a shot –

MEG. I know you would. You don't have to tell me. In the old days, if I caught so much as a cold, you'd start packing your suitcase. Good job it's not me who's disabled, isn't it? You'd be long gone. I'd be trapped here all on my own, wouldn't I?

MICKY. *(Gloomily.)* It's me that's trapped, isn't it? I'm the one who's trapped.

(MEG goes off again.)

MEG. *(As she goes.)* Rubbish. You're not trapped. You've got me here. You're perfectly free to move around if you want.

MICKY. *(Calling.)* Move around? Have you seen the state of my legs lately, have you?

MEG. I see them every single morning, don't I, when I put your stockings on. I'm sick of the sight of your legs.

MICKY. *(Sulkily.)* You don't have to do it.

(MEG returns this time with a plate of small cakes and some fancy biscuits.)

MEG. *(As she enters.)* Yes, I do have to do it. Else you'd be even more trapped. Doctor said those legs would swell up like balloons without your stockings. No, I miss Faith, sometimes, popping in to have a little moan. I hope we see her kids again, too. Little Colin and Christine. I grew quite fond of them, as well. Mind you, I say little Colin, he'll be nearly twenty now, won't he?

MICKY. Adrian adored them, didn't he? Devoted. Even if they weren't his.

MEG. It was mutual. Such a shame. Still, she's only staying at her mother's – *(As she goes.)* You never know, we may not have seen the last of her.

(MEG goes off again.)

MICKY. *(Muttering.)* I hope to God we have.

MEG. *(Offstage.)* No, I have to say, this new one sounds quite promising.

MICKY. *(Calling.)* Where'd he meet her, then?

MEG. *(Offstage.)* At a church coffee morning, apparently.

MICKY. *(Calling.)* Church coffee morning? What's Adrian doing at a church coffee morning?

MEG. *(Offstage.)* No, he's gone a little bit religious lately. Joined the local church, he told me.

MICKY. What? In Nottingham?

MEG. *(Returning.)* I don't know if he's gone religious or just got a bit lonely. Wanted to meet new people, you know. Women.

(MEG has brought in a tray with four cups together with the mats for the tea pot, etc.)

MICKY. What kind of woman's he going to meet at a church coffee morning?

MEG. Well, hopefully, a nice, pleasant, well-spoken one, like this Grace.

MICKY. So long as she's cheerful. Most of those churchgoers, in my experience, they turn out right miserable buggers.

MICKY. *(Dubiously.)* Well. It's worth a try. He's had a go almost everywhere else, hasn't he? Pubs, social clubs, internet dating. Everywhere. Last resort really, isn't it, the church?

(MEG goes off again.)

MEG. *(As she goes.)* It was good of the neighbours to come round this morning, wasn't it? The neighbours?

MICKY. *(Without enthusiasm, calling.)* Very nice of them.

MEG. *(Offstage.)* Neighbourly. All stood out on the front lawn there, singing happy birthday through the window. It was lovely.

MICKY. *(To himself.)* Bloody racket.

MEG. *(Offstage.)* And then leaving you all those presents, which you don't deserve.

MICKY. *(Glaring at the side table, muttering.)* Which I never even asked for.

> (**MEG** *returns with an empty cake stand. She finally places this on the table and, during the next, arranges things in their final positions.*)

MEG. *(As she enters.)* It was good of them. 'specially since you never speak to most of them half the time. Always left to me, isn't it? You never even thanked them properly, did you? Not so much as a smile.

MICKY. I'm not smiling at that lot. Can't stand half of them, anyway.

MEG. Well, you can say that now. We'd be glad of them in an emergency, wouldn't we? Our neighbours? Say we fell down and couldn't get up again...

MICKY. What, both of us?

MEG. ...supposing I slipped on that bathroom floor, say, like nearly happened the other day, on the wet? Supposing I slipped over, and you fell on top of me? So neither of us could get up again? What would happen then?

MICKY. We'd be buggered, wouldn't we?

MEG. We'd be glad of them then. We'd be grateful for neighbours then, wouldn't we? *(Surveying the table.)*

I won't bring the cake in, not just yet. We'll wait till they're here.

MICKY. Oh, we've got cake, have we?

MEG. 'course we've got cake. It wouldn't be a birthday without cake, would it? I made one specially.

MICKY. What sort of cake?

MEG. Wait and see. Surprise.

MICKY. Not full of nuts and fruit, is it? You know I can't eat nuts and fruit, they get stuck under my plate.

MEG. It's a perfectly plain lemon sponge with a soft butter icing. I remembered, don't worry. I don't want you taking your teeth out in the middle of tea again, not in front of Grace.

MICKY. Where's Sonia, then? Is Sonia coming?

MEG. No, I told you this morning, they're still in Spain. She's working. So's Peter. They're both working. They can't get away, till the weekend, I told you that.

MICKY. They're always working, her and Peter. Both of them at it, non-stop.

MEG. Thank your lucky stars we've got a successful daughter and son-in-law, to take care of us in emergencies. At least we've got one successful child. Count your blessings. We'd be in real trouble if we had to rely on just Adrian, wouldn't we?

MICKY. Oh, don't start getting at him, again...

MEG. Well, stuck in that dead-end job at Dunstan's. How long's he been there, now? Thirty years, isn't it? Over thirty years, must be.

MICKY. He's doing well. Head of his department now, isn't he?

MEG. Assistant head. He's only the assistant.

MICKY. Well, he's got another ten years yet. If he sticks at it, he could well be head, by the time he retires.

MEG. He used to have so many plans, didn't he? When he was young? Such big ambitions. What was it he wanted to be at one time? An astrophysicist, didn't he? Now what is he? A bookkeeper at Dunstan's Department store.

MICKY. *(Gloomily.)* Ah, well, he had to come down to earth eventually, didn't he? We all start out with ambitions. I did. Never thought I'd end up as a coach driver. Not my original dream, was that, ferrying busloads of drunks to and fro across the country.

MEG. *(Rather sadly.)* I always wanted to be a dance teacher, at one time. Have my own dancing school. Always my dream, that. And then I ended up sitting behind a till at Sainsbury's, didn't I?

MICKY. You were better off sitting behind a till, believe me. Far better off.

MEG. Think so?

MICKY. Else you wouldn't have met me, would you? You'd never have caught me going into a bloody dancing school, I can tell you.

MEG. No, that'd be the day. Anyway, they'll be here at the weekend, Sonia, Peter and the kids. Then we're all out to dinner on Saturday, aren't we? Don't worry, they're paying. I booked us in at The Plough. They're good with kiddies. Remember you enjoyed The Plough last time, didn't you?

MICKY. That the one with the steak and kidney?

MEG. That's the one. And then you had the crumble. Remember you 'specially liked their crumble? You had seconds, didn't you? And most of mine too, on top of that.

MICKY. *(Savouring.)* Oh, aye, the crumble!

MEG. You were up and down all night after, weren't you?

MICKY. Good apple crumble, that. Steak and kidney pie and apple crumble. That's me sorted, then.

MEG. Remind me to stock up on the Rennies.

(Another pause.)

MICKY. You think we ought to warn her, then?

MEG. What?

MICKY. This new woman of Adrian's? You think we should warn her?

MEG. Grace? Warn her of what?

MICKY. About Adrian? About his predilections? You know. These personality shifts of his?

MEG. *(Firmly.)* I don't think we need say anything about that.

MICKY. We don't want it happening again, do we?

MEG. Not a single word. Listen, it's just a theory. It's just a crackpot theory of yours –

MICKY. More than a theory –

MEG. – we don't know it for certain –

MICKY. – it's a fact. And with her being a churchgoer, religious and so on, she might be, you know, more vulnerable. Sensitive –

MEG. – we don't need to say anything –

MICKY. – it's the problem with his personality, isn't it? That's what broke up his other relationships, wasn't it –?

MEG. – we don't know that –

MICKY. – it's what broke up his marriage. Faith said, in so many words. The reason it all broke down. On account of his – insatiable demands, you know –

MEG. – we don't know that for certain. That's just your interpretation –

MICKY. – we owe it to – this – Grace, don't we? Wouldn't be fair on her, would it? We need to get in early this time. Nip it in the bud. Fair to her, fair to both of them. Else the lad's never going to form a proper relationship with a woman, ever again, is he? That's my opinion.

MEG. Yes, it is, it's just your opinion. That's all it is. Personally, I don't think we should say anything to her. It's not our place to interfere.

MICKY. We're his parents, we owe it to him.

MEG. *(Resolutely.)* Well, I'm not saying a word. This time I'm not saying a single word. I'm sorry, Micky, but I think all this interfering in the lad's life, it's doing more harm than good, it really is.

MICKY. He's ill. He's imbalanced. Partly mental, partly hormones. He's got unbalanced hormones. They're out of kilter.

MEG. What are you on about now? Hormones? I think you're beginning to lose it, love, I really do. You're going bonkers on your birthday.

MICKY. No, listen. Superman. You remember Superman?

MEG. Oh, for God's sake don't start on again about Superman –

MICKY. No, listen, listen to me –

MEG. – every time we get on this subject, you bring up bloody Superman. I don't know what he's got to do with Adrian's sexual problems – I think you're going off your head, Micky. It's your age, love, it's got to you –

MICKY. – nothing wrong with my head –

MEG. Listen, if you honestly believe we've got Superman as a son…take a look at him. Just take a look at Adrian, the next time you see him. He's a lovely gentle lad and I won't have a word said against him, but really! I can't imagine anybody less like bloody Superman than Adrian Copthorpe! Now shut up or I'll have you put away.

(A slight pause.)

MICKY. *(Muttering.)* The lass needs warning, that's all I'm saying, she needs warning.

MEG. That's enough! Or I promise. They'll be round here with a van!

(Another pause.)

MICKY. Should be here by now, shouldn't they?

MEG. There might be traffic. If they're coming from Nottingham. It's never good between here and Nottingham, not on a Friday. 'Specially if Adrian's driving. It'll take even longer with him at the wheel. In the old days, whenever he took me to the shops, he'd drive so slowly. I'd say, Adrian, for God's sake get a move on, love, they'll all be closed. He'd stop for everything. He only had to see a crossing sign and he'd slam his brakes on, even when there was no one there…

MICKY. He's a responsible, conscientious driver. I taught him well.

MEG. …one time, he even pulled up for a pile of leaves. I said, Adrian, they're just leaves, love, off the trees. It's perfectly safe to run them over.

MICKY. …there should be more drivers like him on our roads, if you ask me.

MEG. Now you're alright sitting there, are you? You need anything bringing, before they come?

MICKY. Just my tea.

MEG. You'll get it in a minute. Soon as they arrive. You're still dry, are you? You're not damp?

MICKY. No, I'm dry enough.

MEG. Only I don't want you sitting there feeling uncomfortable. Not on your birthday.

MICKY. No, I'm alright just now. Comfortable enough.

(Another pause.)

MEG. I've sorted out a parking disc. Put one on the hall table for them.

MICKY. They'll need one, if they're here more than five minutes. You know what those buggers are like...

MEG. Uncle Hal's Jaguar. He hadn't been parked two minutes, had he? And they swooped just like that. Threatened to tow him away, didn't they?

MICKY. Mind you, out of date licence, no tax disc and three bald tyres, what did he expect? But then that's Hal for you, isn't it?

MEG. Oh, yes, that's Hal for you.

MICKY. Bloody black sheep, wasn't he, your brother?

MEG. Well, he's passed on now. To a better place.

MICKY. He'll be lucky to get there. Not with three bald tyres and no tax disc.

(The doorbell rings.)

MEG. Oh, they're here!

(She hurries to the front window to check.)

Yes, it's them. Now, remember, behave yourself!

MICKY. How do you mean?

MEG. None of that Superman nonsense, you hear?

>(**MEG** *hurries out to the front door.*)

MICKY. (*Muttering to himself again.*) Something needs to be said. She needs warning, the lass needs warning.

>(**MEG** *is heard greeting their guests in the hall. In a moment,* **ADRIAN** *and* **GRACE** *are ushered in by* **MEG**. **ADRIAN** *is very much as described. A mild, undistinguished man in his mid-fifties.* **GRACE**, *ten years his junior, is similarly well-disposed with a sunny, unassuming manner, currently a little shy.* **ADRIAN** *immediately bounds forward to greet his father. He is carrying a gift-wrapped book.*)

ADRIAN. (*Affectionately.*) Hello, Dad. Happy birthday, mate.

MICKY. (*Brightly.*) Adrian, son! How's it all going?

ADRIAN. (*Handing him the book.*) Here. Happy birthday.

MICKY. Oh. You shouldn't have bothered, lad.

MEG. (*Stepping forward.*) Here, I'll take it. I'll put it over here with his other presents, he can open it later.

ADRIAN. It's a Pictorial History of The Omnibus.

MICKY. Oh, aye.

MEG. Oh, doesn't that sound lovely. Very interesting.

ADRIAN. I had to send away for it especially. There's some fascinating old pictures. I think you'll appreciate it, Dad.

MICKY. I'm sure.

ADRIAN. You're looking good. Looking good, Dad. How are you feeling in yourself?

MICKY. Oh, pretty fair. Considering.

ADRIAN. He's looking great, isn't he, Mum? Don't you think he's looking good?

MEG. He's doing alright. Not bad for eighty.

(A slight pause.)

Come on, then, Adrian. Aren't you going to introduce Grace to your Dad? Where's your manners?

ADRIAN. Oh, yes, sure. Sorry. Grace, this is my Dad.

GRACE. *(Shyly.)* How do you do, Mr Copthorpe?

MICKY. Micky, love, call me Micky. Now I'm eighty you can call me Micky.

GRACE. Congratulations. Happy birthday

MEG. And I'm Meg, love. Do call me Meg, please.

GRACE. Meg. Oh, isn't this a lovely cosy room! It's so lovely and cosy, isn't it?

MEG. Well, thank you. I don't know about cosy, I think poky is how we usually describe it, isn't it, Micky?

GRACE. No, really, it's just so warm and welcoming. I love the colours.

ADRIAN. *(At the side table.)* Hey, look at all these presents! These all for you, are they, Dad?

MICKY. Hands off! Hands off, you bugger!

ADRIAN. Who's being spoilt on his birthday, then?

MEG. Now, Grace, do sit down, make yourself comfortable, love. I was just about to put the kettle on, make us all a nice cup of tea.

GRACE. Oh, wonderful.

MEG. I bet you're dying for a cup of tea, aren't you? After your journey?

GRACE. Lovely.

MEG. How was your journey? You've made good time, haven't you?

ADRIAN. Oh, it was good, wasn't it? Pretty clear. Less on the road than usual.

MICKY. No piles of leaves, then?

ADRIAN. Sorry?

MEG. *(Gently admonishing.)* Micky! Behave!

ADRIAN. Piles of leaves?

MEG. I'll just heat the kettle up.

GRACE. Can I help at all?

MEG. No, it's all ready to bring in. I've just got to warm the kettle.

GRACE. *(Following her to the door.)* Do let me help, please. I'd love to see the kitchen.

MEG. *(As they leave.)* Well, I'm afraid it's a bit of a mess at present...

GRACE. *(Going with her.)* Oh, that's alright, don't worry. You should see my kitchen...

(**MEG** *and* **GRACE** *leave the room.*)

ADRIAN. *(At the main table.)* Hey! Look at all this. One of mum's teas. Eat till you drop, eh? Where's the cake then? We're getting a cake, surely?

MICKY. It's out there. Saving itself for the grand finale.

ADRIAN. Has it got eighty candles?

MICKY. I hope not. There'll be more bloody candles than cake.

ADRIAN. *(With a glance towards the kitchen.)* Well, leave them both to it, eh? Get to know each other. What do you think of her then, Dad? Grace? From what you've seen? Gorgeous, isn't she?

MICKY. *(Guardedly.)* She seems – very pleasant. Course, I've only just...

ADRIAN. Oh, wait till you get to know her, Dad. She's special. Grace's really special. I think she's the one this time, Dad, I really do. I think I've found her at last. The one I want to share the rest of my life with. She's just – perfect. Kind and gentle. Understanding. She's a really – good person – you know. In the real sense.

MICKY. Yes, I heard she was a – she's a Christian, isn't she?

ADRIAN. Yes. She's a Christian. But in the proper sense, you know. Not one of those do-gooder, holier than thou sort of Christians. A proper Christian with love in her heart. Not just for me. For everyone around her. Whenever she walks in, she just lights the place up. Like a three-thousand-watt bulb. Dad, you've no idea, I'm such a happy man. I'm seventeen years old again, walking on air.

MICKY. Well, I'm happy for you, son, I really am. You deserve a bit of happiness. You've been through a bit. I'm pleased for you.

ADRIAN. *(Grasping his hand.)* Thank you, Dad. Thank you. That means a lot. Bless you.

MICKY. But, being absolutely straight for a minute, son. And if I sound – if I sound a bit less than – over the moon for you – it's just we've been down this path once or twice before, haven't we? I mean, only in recent months, haven't we? I mean, truthfully, this isn't the first one you've said that about, is it?

ADRIAN. No, this is different. This time it's definitely different. I'm positive. It's the real thing, this time.

MICKY. I mean, I don't want to put a damper on your happiness, but – Adrian, if you'll take a bit of advice from your dad...

ADRIAN. Of course, of course...

MICKY. I mean, I may not be what you'd call the wisest of people, you know –

ADRIAN. Oh, yes you are, Dad. To me anyway, you are –

MICKY. – but I have lived to be eighty and so I may have picked up a thing or two, over the years, with regards to women.

ADRIAN. I'm sure you have, Dad.

MICKY. Rule one with women. Don't try and rush them, son. In my experience, women mostly prefer to set the pace – you don't mind me saying this to you, do you –?

ADRIAN. *(Considering this, gravely.)* No, well, they're wise words, Dad. Words of wisdom. You know me, I never tend to rush things. Kid gloves, me.

MICKY. Treat her like your best bone china. Don't be like your mother's brother.

ADRIAN. You mean Uncle Hal?

MICKY. Don't get like him. He's wrecked havoc in his wake, that man. Left a trail of broken hearts behind him. Don't get like him, lad.

ADRIAN. Yes, Mum's sixtieth birthday, at the Swan? Remember when he –?

MICKY. Don't mention that. Not in front of your mother, son!

ADRIAN. Yes, I remember when Mum went and – *(He breaks off.)*

*(**MEG** and **GRACE** return with the tea things.)*

MEG. Sorry. We got nattering. Yatter, yatter, yatter...

MICKY. Oh, yes? Why are we not surprised?

MEG. We've been discussing wallpaper, of all things. I don't know how we got on to wallpaper, do you, Grace?

GRACE. We started on lino. Old-fashioned lino. How we wished they'd bring it back, instead of all these fancy tiles that always need specialist people to lay them. Whereas, a good old-fashioned roll of lino, you can lay it yourself, can't you?

MEG. They must still make lino, mustn't they?

GRACE. You just never see it though, do you?

MICKY. I wouldn't know.

MEG. Anyway, enough of that. Tea, everybody? Everyone wants tea, I take it?

ADRIAN. Please.

GRACE. Lovely.

MEG. Micky?

MICKY. What?

MEG. You want a cup of tea, love, don't you?

MICKY. Ta.

MEG. So, what have you two been talking about in here?

ADRIAN. We were just remembering your sixtieth birthday at the Swan.

MEG. Oh, don't bring that up again, please.

GRACE. Why's that?

MEG. Never a year goes by without him bringing that up. I thought we'd forgotten all about that.

GRACE. Whatever happened?

ADRIAN. Well, Mum –

MEG. Don't you dare! Not one word, my boy! Unless you want this tea poured over your head. I'll tell you some time when we're on our own, Grace. Once we know you a little better. Would you mind passing those. Thank you.

(**GRACE** *passes cups to both the men.*)

MICKY. Ta.

ADRIAN. Thank you.

(**MEG** *pours* **GRACE** *a cup.*)

GRACE. *(Taking her cup.)* Thank you.

MEG. You don't take sugar, do you, Grace?

GRACE. No, thank you.

ADRIAN. *(Smiling at her.)* Sweet enough already, aren't you?

(**GRACE** *smiles back at him.*)

(**MEG** *sits at the table and pours herself a cup as well.*)

(*Meanwhile* **ADRIAN** *has sat on the sofa.*)

(**GRACE,** *taking her own cup, crosses companionably to sit next to him.*)

(**GRACE** *smiles at* **ADRIAN.** *He smiles back at her.*)

MEG. Well, isn't this nice? Micky's birthday tea. We should give him a toast, really. Only I don't think it's the done thing to toast someone with tea, is it? *(Raising her cup.)* A toast anyway. To Micky. And many more to come, love.

GRACE. *(Raising her cup.)* Micky!

ADRIAN. *(Raising his cup.)* To Dad!

> *(They all drink.)*

MEG. *(With a yelp of alarm.)* Oh, my God! I completely forgot. You haven't done your parking disc, Adrian.

ADRIAN. *(Springing up.)* Oh, no. Forgot that. Must do that.

MICKY. No, don't forget your disc. You know what they're like round here.

ADRIAN. I'll do it straightaway. Won't be a tick.

MEG. Are you parked far away?

ADRIAN. *(As he goes.)* Just round the corner in Park Street. Won't be long!

> *(**ADRIAN** hurries out.)*

MEG. *(Calling after him.)* It's just on the hall table there.

ADRIAN. *(Offstage.)* Got it!

MICKY. *(To **GRACE**.)* They're 'specially fierce round here. Adrian's uncle Hal, my wife's brother, he had a serious altercation with his Jaguar.

GRACE. Oh, yes?

MEG. *(Calling.)* Adrian, leave it on the latch, love.

ADRIAN. *(Offstage.)* Right!

MICKY. *(Significantly.)* Three bald tyres and no tax disc...

GRACE. *(Laughing.)* Oh, really? That's incredible.

> *(**MEG** removes the cling film from the plate of sandwiches.)*
>
> *(In a moment, the front door closes.)*

MEG. Well, we won't wait for Adrian. Something to eat, everyone?

(**GRACE** *rises and takes the side plates from the table.*)

GRACE. I'll pass these round, shall I?

MEG. Oh, thank you, love, if you wouldn't mind. Terrible asking guests to do it, but…

GRACE. Quite alright, happy to help.

(*She distributes the plates, leaving one by* **MICKY** *and two others by the sofa for her and* **ADRIAN.**)

(*Indicating the plates of sandwiches.*) Would you like me to do these as well?

MEG. Thank you, love. (*Indicating.*) Those are the paste. And those there are cucumber. (*Confidentially.*) Only don't give Micky any cucumber. They interfere with him.

(**GRACE** *now offers* **MICKY** *the paste sandwiches. He takes two.*)

(*She takes two sandwiches for herself and two for* **ADRIAN.**)

(*She returns both plates to the main table for* **MEG** *to help herself.*)

(*During this, the conversation continues.*)

So how did you and Adrian meet, Grace?

GRACE. (*As she busies herself.*) We met at a coffee morning. A St Catherine's Church coffee morning. One of those Saturday morning do's. You know. Rather sad actually. All the people in the parish with nowhere else to go on Saturday morning. A bit of a lonely-hearts club, really. And Adrian and I found we both had a lot in common, being both of us on our own. With his wife having – only recently left him, you know.

MEG. And you'd been in a relationship of your own before, as well?

GRACE. No, no. Goodness no. I was entirely on my own. Always have been.

MEG. What, always?

GRACE. Well, yes, basically. Yes. The occasional boyfriend. Occasionally. Very occasional. Sort of boyfriends, anyway. If you could even call them boyfriends. Middle-aged-men-friends, really. Nothing, you know, that deep. Nothing really lasting or permanent. Not really.

MEG. Let's hope this works out better for you.

GRACE. We live in hope. So far so good. We're moving quite carefully, both of us, determined not to rush into things. Adrian's being particularly cautious, you know, after his unfortunate marriage. Certainly, from my side, anyway, it's all going swimmingly. Quite slowly but... I can't really speak for Adrian, of course.

MEG. He seems very happy, too. So far as you can tell from Adrian. Wouldn't you say so, Micky?

MICKY. What's that?

MEG. Adrian? He seems happy, doesn't he? Just at present?

MICKY. Oh, yes. He's happy.

GRACE. *(Sitting back on the sofa.)* Still, we'll have to see, won't we? Early days, yet. Time will tell, won't it?

MICKY. *(Grimly.)* Aye, it certainly will. Plenty of time still, isn't there?

GRACE. Yes, I wish there was. But we're both of us "of an age" as they say. So. I sort of feel – clock's ticking and so on. I feel Adrian still hasn't quite got over his marriage. He hasn't quite got over Faith leaving him. I think that's what's holding him back, really. When we first met, I asked him what had brought him there because I hadn't seen him there before. And he told me, he was there because he'd lost faith. Only he meant his wife Faith, of course. Which made me laugh when he explained it, because I thought it was really rather witty. Only I don't think he was joking. Not at all. Probably tactless of me, laughing like that. But then I do tend to laugh rather too much. Or so people tell me. My defensive default position, really. If I don't understand something people are saying, I do tend to laugh. Probably not an awfully good habit, especially with regard to men, is it? They tend not to like it if you laugh in the wrong places. They usually prefer to control the jokes, men do. Not that Adrian's like that. Not at all. But at the end of it all, I do feel, he still misses his wife, you know. He's holding back something. He's not, you know, yet prepared to fully commit. But, you know, we live in hope. *(She laughs.)*

MEG. No, well, you can't rush Adrian, he won't be rushed. Not in the normal course of events. I hope he gets over his marriage, though. It didn't end happily, I have to say. Faith wasn't happy, not by the end.

MICKY. Miserable. She was a complete and utter misery.

GRACE. And what do you think could have caused it? I mean, it couldn't possibly have been postnatal, could it?

MEG. Oh, no, she came with the children from a previous marriage. Christine was five and little Colin was three by the time she married Adrian. She must have got over all that by the time they married. It couldn't have possibly been postnatal.

GRACE. No. Odd.

MEG. I think it was just part of her nature. It was in her nature.

GRACE. Yes.

(A slight pause whilst they consider this.)

MICKY. It was him.

GRACE. Sorry?

MICKY. He was entirely to blame.

GRACE. You mean her first husband?

MICKY. No, Adrian. He caused her depression. He wore her out.

MEG. Micky!

GRACE. How do you mean exactly? Wore her out?

MICKY. He made unnatural demands on her, the lass couldn't cope. She hadn't the stamina.

GRACE. What?

MEG. Now, Micky, that's enough of that. We agreed, didn't we –?

MICKY. No, she needs to know, Meg. I'm sorry, I need to speak out. This woman needs to know the truth!

MEG. She doesn't want to sit here listening to your ridiculous theories.

MICKY. They're founded in fact. Hard fact. Backed up by witnesses.

GRACE. *(Laughing.)* I'm not quite following this, I'm afraid. What are these unnatural demands? Are we talking about physical demands?

MICKY. Oh, aye. It was physical alright. He wore her down. Perfectly strong healthy woman, when they were wed, and then in two years, worn down to a shadow of her former self –

MEG. *(Brightly.)* You know, the problem I have with these modern wallpapers, Grace, is these firms keep changing their patterns. The minute you get one you like, that you're really fond of, they discontinue it –

MICKY. She was a wraith. A walking wraith, Grace. Time he'd finished with her.

GRACE. You're saying, she couldn't cope with his sexual demands?

MICKY. If you want to put it that crudely.

MEG. So, then it's impossible to get a match with your original paper. So, you just have to start again, don't you? With a fresh pattern. It's so frustrating –

MICKY. I'm telling you, Grace, that lad's got two sides to him. The one you see, day-to-day like, and then his other dark side he keeps hidden from the world –

MEG. Because then, of course, you've nothing else which matches with it, have you –?

MICKY. It's hormones. He's got unbalanced hormones. They're out of kilter –

MEG. Not your curtains, your carpets, your loose covers, nothing –

MICKY. Listen, Grace, you remember Superman, do you?

MEG. *(Despairingly.)* Micky, for God's sake don't start!

GRACE. *(Laughing nervously.)* Yes, I remember Superman –

MEG. Don't get him started, Grace, don't get him started –

GRACE. What's Superman got to do with Adrian?

MICKY. You recall normally he was a mild-mannered bloke, Clark Kent, very much like Adrian, but the first hint of trouble –

MEG. Micky! Will you stop this?

MICKY. Don't interrupt, I'm talking, I'm telling her – at the first hint of trouble, he'd run into his phone box and he'd whirl round, change and shazam! He'd come out of his phone box as Superman!

MEG. I can't bear it! Don't listen to this, Grace, he's completely mad.

MICKY. And that is precisely what happens to Adrian, Grace. Sexually.

GRACE. *(Laughing a lot now.)* Heavens! You can't be serious?

MEG. He's not serious. He's completely mad.

MICKY. Alright, you tell her about what happened on his thirtieth. Tell Grace what happened on Adrian's thirtieth birthday. You were there. Tell her.

MEG. No, don't start on that!

GRACE. What happened on his thirtieth birthday?

MICKY. Adrian was living away in Nottingham in a flat on his own. So we assumed he was going to be spending his birthday on his own, didn't we...?

MEG. Micky! Don't go on with this, please!

MICKY. ...him having no regular partner, like. So we both drove over 'specially to surprise him. And when we rang his bell, there was him and this naked call girl –

GRACE. Good gracious!

MEG. This is total rubbish, this is totally untrue –

MICKY. – both of them, Grace, out of their skulls. Drunk as a couple of skunks on vodka.

GRACE. But Adrian never drinks. He's teetotal.

MICKY. Ah. That's the Adrian you know, Grace. But this other Adrian, he drinks himself to a standstill. *(To* **MEG.***)* That's how it was, wasn't it? I'm not lying, am I?

(**GRACE** *looks at* **MEG**.)

MEG. *(Reluctantly.)* That was vaguely how it was, yes.

MICKY. No, Meg. That was exactly how it was. Exactly. That girl, Grace, she were a hardened pro, you could tell she was. But, sparing your feelings, Grace, I know you're a churchgoer and I'm sorry for putting it like this, but that lass after two hours with Adrian was completely knackered. Dead on her feet.

GRACE. *(Stunned.)* Dear heavens!

MICKY. Mind you, she said it were the best, the most satisfying couple of hours she'd ever had in her life. And that were from the mouth of a pro, Grace.

GRACE. Good Lord!

MEG. It was just unfortunate, it happened to be that particular day –

MICKY. For all we know, he was doing that on a daily basis! How do we know she was the only one? Probably one a day. Or three at a time, for all we know.

MEG. Yes, love, now, getting back to the subject in hand, we were talking about wallpaper, weren't we, Grace?

GRACE. *(Still a little dazed.)* Were we?

MEG. As I was saying, we had this matching problem, didn't we, Micky? In the dining room with the striped one was bad enough. And then, as for the bedrooms. We had this terrible trouble with Sonia's, didn't we, Micky? She was so attached to that original paper, she was destitute. And as for Adrian's room, that was a nightmare, too.

MICKY. Mind you, that room of Adrian's could tell a tale or two. If it so wished.

MEG. What are you talking about, now?

MICKY. Sonia's eighteenth. Her eighteenth birthday party, remember?

MEG. No! That's quite enough! We're not going into all that now, either. He was seventeen, that's all it was. Besides, we don't even know if it's true, we've only got Sonia's word for it, haven't we?

MICKY. She was pretty definite about it. It was with Sonia's best friend. His sister was having a few girlfriends round to celebrate, you know –

> (**MEG** *rises abruptly and moves to the window.*)

MEG. I don't know where he's got to. He only had to walk round the corner –

MICKY. ...and this is according to his sister Sonia, Adrian lures her best friend up into his room and takes advantage of her in his wardrobe...

GRACE. This just doesn't sound like Adrian, not at all. Why on earth would he take her in the wardrobe?

MICKY. As I say, two sides, Grace, he's got two sides. My theory is the reason he chose the wardrobe was in order to stifle her cries. (*Nodding towards* **MEG**.) But his mother doesn't care to talk about it.

MEG. (*Still at the window.*) There's no sign of him. Where on earth's he got to?

GRACE. (*Laughing.*) I have to say, I'd never have guessed. It's a side of him I never knew existed. I'm a bit stunned. I can't believe we're talking about the same Adrian, I really can't.

MICKY. Jekyll and Hyde, love. Thank your lucky stars, so far, you've only met Dr Jekyll. Pray God you don't run into Mr Hyde.

GRACE. (*Laughing.*) I think on the whole I prefer Superman.

MEG. Oh, there he is! He's got talking to someone, that's what it is. Oh, it's that town councillor, used to be mayor, Councillor Mrs Packham. Lived round here at one time. Her parents ran the off-licence on the corner. She moved to Cragg Top along with the rest of the council.

MICKY. They don't have problems with parking up at Cragg Top, do they?

MEG. *(Rapping on the window, calling.)* Adrian! Adrian! Come in! Come in! Your tea's stone cold! *(To them.)* Yes, she used to live just down the street. Friend of Sonia's. Hope Packham. Used to be Hope Smith.

MICKY. Hope Smith! That was it!! That were the one in the cupboard!

GRACE. *(Moving rapidly to the window.)* Was she?

MEG. Yes, that woman over there. The – you're not supposed to say it these days, are you? – the portly one, Councillor Packham.

MICKY. Council fat cats.

> *(The front door slams.)*
>
> *(They move away from the window.)*
>
> *(**ADRIAN** enters.)*

ADRIAN. *(As he enters.)* Sorry. Got talking to someone.

MEG. We saw you. That was Councillor Packham, wasn't it?

ADRIAN. Yes. Used to live just down the road. Haven't seen her for ages. Not since I moved away. *(To **GRACE**.)* Hello, love, alright, are you?

GRACE. Fine. I'm fine.

ADRIAN. Now then, where's my tea?

MEG. It's been standing there for ages. It'll be stone cold by now. Wait a moment, I'll pour you some fresh. Then we must have the cake, mustn't we? Light the candle. I'm afraid I only got the one candle.

MICKY. Before we do that, love, I think I'm in urgent need of the facilities. Tea went straight through me.

MEG. Oh, right. *(Moving to him.)* Let's get you moving then – Adrian, would you mind? Help your dad up, would you?

ADRIAN. *(Moving in to help.)* Yes, of course.

MEG. Just give him your hand, love. That's all he needs. One firm heave.

MICKY. *(Hauling himself up.)* Hup!

ADRIAN. Hup! That's it! There you go!

>*(MICKY stands stiffly.)*

MEG. I can take it from here. I can manage from here. Thank you. *(To MICKY.)* OK? Can you hold it?

MICKY. I can hold it.

MEG. Here we go then. One, two, three...

>*(MEG steers MICKY speedily to the door. It is an experienced manoeuvre.)*

MICKY. *(As they go.)* Bloody tea. Goes straight through you.

MEG. *(As she steers him.)* He needs steering, he needs steering along here. He had that barometer off the wall the other day...

>*(MEG and MICKY go off.)*

>*(ADRIAN finds his tea and drinks it in one gulp.)*

GRACE. That must be horrible by now.

ADRIAN. *(Grimacing.)* It was a bit. Wet and lukewarm, anyway.

> (**GRACE** *takes the cup from him and returns it to the table.*)

So, have Mum and Dad been keeping you amused?

GRACE. They've been – reminiscing, you know.

ADRIAN. About me?

GRACE. Yes.

ADRIAN. Oh, dear. What have they been saying? I dread to think.

> (*He sits on the sofa.*)

Did they drag out the baby pictures, then?

GRACE. No, not quite.

ADRIAN. You were spared them at least.

GRACE. *(Sitting beside him.)* Yes, I was spared them.

> (*A pause. She stares at him.*)

ADRIAN. *(A little embarrassed by this scrutiny.)* What's wrong? Anything wrong?

GRACE. No, I'm just re-examining you. Through fresh eyes.

> (*She continues to scrutinise him.*)

ADRIAN. *(Somewhat nervously, continuing.)* I was just thinking what we might do when we leave here, if you're up for it, that is. Rather than drive straight back, there's one or two quite pleasant little restaurants not too far away, I think they'll still be here. I thought we could try one of those. That's if you're up for it, of course. I don't want to take up too much more of your day. It's very good of you to have come with me in the first place. But it would be nice, don't you think, if we could both just...sit down together and have a...chat... just a chat, you know, nothing more than that. I don't know how you feel about that really, I – *(He tails off.)* Sorry? What is it?

GRACE. I'm sorry. I'm sorry, Adrian, I've waited long enough. I'm forty-five years old and I can't wait a minute longer. I'm so sorry.

> (**GRACE** *suddenly launches herself at him, clamping her mouth to his in a sudden, violent, unexpected kiss.*)

> (**ADRIAN**, *taken by surprise, is knocked backwards by this and* **GRACE**, *now half on top of him, transfers her kissing to include the rest of his face, whilst her arms, somewhat feverishly, explore his body.*)

ADRIAN. *(Coming up for air.)* Grace? Grace! What are you doing? What the hell are you doing?

GRACE. *(Frenziedly continuing.)* ...Come on... Come on, then... Come on, come on, come on, then...

ADRIAN. *(Trying to extricate himself.)* Grace, please don't, we mustn't, we can't, not here...

GRACE. ...come on, why can't you, COME ON! *(With a cry of frustration.)* Come out of your fucking phone box!

> (**ADRIAN** *finally manages to prise himself free.*)

> (*He wriggles from under her and retreats, backing across the floor away from her. He retreats as far as the tea table.*)

> (*She starts to stalk him, animal-like, a woman possessed.*)

ADRIAN. *(As he retreats from her in desperation.)* What are you talking about? Why do you all keep going on about phone boxes? What's all this with phone boxes?

GRACE. *(Smiling savagely.)* Come on, then, Superman! Shazam!

> *(She launches herself at him once more, this time knocking him backwards and causing him to grab the tea table behind him for support, the gate leg section of which promptly collapses.)*

> *(**GRACE** grabs him again by the front of his jacket and pulls him down so he lands on top of her. He struggles ineffectually to free himself, but she maintains a steely grip. At this point, **MICKY** and **MEG** return. She, steers him with one hand and in the other she balances his birthday cake with a single burning candle.)*

MICKY. *(In triumph.)* See that? He's out again! He's out again, love!

> *(As they take in the scene, the lights fade to:)*

> *(Blackout.)*

End of Scene One

Scene Two

*(**MEG**'s sixtieth. Fifteen years ago. A small private side room off the ballroom of The Swan Hotel. Just about to get underway is a surprise private party for **MEG**, arranged by **MICKY**. The room we are in currently is intended tonight to be a retiring room, for the birthday girl and her immediate family. There are two doors, one leading out into the main hotel, the other opening directly onto the ballroom itself where the main body of fifty or so guests are gathered. In this room, various soft furnishings, well-used armchairs, sofas etc. and at least one table with two upright chairs.)*

*(Currently, **ADRIAN** is standing alone, waiting. He is now forty years of age but looks much the same. In a moment, the ballroom door opens and there is a brief burst of subdued conversation as **MICKY**, now aged sixty-five, enters. He backs on, addressing the unseen assembled guests as he does so.)*

MICKY. ...she's – she's just doing a bit of final titivating, she'll be with us in just a moment. But I must stress she's no idea you're here. So, can I ask you all please, for a minute or two, to keep absolutely dead quiet. And then the minute I bring Meg in, Franco, our head waiter over there in the corner, he's going to switch on the main lights and then I want you all to raise your glasses and give her a big warm welcome.

(A murmur from the crowd.)

Sssh! Sssh! Sssh! Completely quiet now, please! Sssh! Not long now. Thank you.

(He finally enters, closing the door behind him.)

(To ADRIAN.*)* No sign of them yet?

ADRIAN. No, they're still in there, presumably.

MICKY. Ah, well. Two women together, what do you expect? Once they get into a toilet, be lucky to see them again, won't we?

ADRIAN. Once those two get talking, certainly.

MICKY. She can natter, yours, can't she? Your Faith? Worse than your mother. I thought she had a mouth on her, but Faith takes some beating.

ADRIAN. She likes to talk, yes. Mostly to other people, though.

MICKY. Well, you're married, aren't you? Not a lot to say to each other, have you? After five years you've just about said it all, haven't you?

ADRIAN. I hope we haven't. I feel, Faith and I – we've still got things left to be said.

MICKY. I can't say your Mum and me have. Mind you, we've been at it longer. Over forty years, us. Not bad, eh, forty years? It's not so difficult. Once you get into a routine, you know. Get used to each other. Over the years. Worst bit's the first twenty. Once you're over that…

ADRIAN. Thanks very much. Can't wait for the next seventeen and a half.

MICKY. No problems, are there? You've not got problems, have you?

ADRIAN. Nothing that we can't – resolve. I hope.

MICKY. I hope you can. You've been married – what? – less than three years, haven't you?

ADRIAN. Two and a half.

MICKY. If you need any advice, son, we're always here for you, your mother and me, you know that.

ADRIAN. Thanks. I think Faith finds it helps sometimes to talk to Meg. Sees her as a sort of second mother, what with Faith's own mother being not that supportive.

MICKY. Remember her at your wedding? Dear oh dear! I can't bear it, you know, seeing a woman in that condition. 'Specially one of her age.

ADRIAN. I think that goes for anybody, doesn't it? Men as well?

MICKY. No, but a woman, 'specially. She needs to maintain her dignity, doesn't she? It's alright for a bloke. He doesn't have much dignity to start with, does he? No, but with a woman, she loses your respect. You need to respect them, don't you?

ADRIAN. Oh, yes.

MICKY. *(With a sudden burst of impatience.)* Where the bloody hell have those two got to?

ADRIAN. Probably still talking.

MICKY. Never mind talking. There's a room full of people in there, holding their breath, standing in the dark, for God's sake.

ADRIAN. Mum doesn't know that though, does she?

MICKY. What?

ADRIAN. Mum doesn't know there's anyone waiting. She thinks it's just us.

MICKY. *(Glaring at his watch.)* I've only paid that bloody disc jockey up till ten thirty, haven't I?

ADRIAN. Bit early to stop, ten thirty, isn't it?

MICKY. Well, I reckon things will have wound down by then. Most of them are me and your mother's age. Well past bedtime for most of us, ten thirty. Pity your sister couldn't make it. Sonia and Peter. She'd have appreciated it, seeing them. Mind you, it was never on the cards, was it? Not from Sri Lanka. I told the disc jockey, don't expect a rave up, mate. Nothing too hectic. Or we'll end up with ambulance crews everywhere. He said he'd pick out some old favourites, you know –

> *(At this point, from the other door,* **MEG**, *dressed in her finery and looking good for sixty enters with* **FAITH**, *a pale, rather drawn woman in her mid-thirties.)*

Oh, hooray, at last!

MEG. *(As they enter.)* Sorry. We got talking.

FAITH. Sorry.

MICKY. We've been waiting here ages.

MEG. Oh, I do beg your pardon, I didn't realise we had a time limit.

MICKY. I mean, you've been fifteen bloody minutes.

MEG. I'm so sorry, I do apologise. Happy birthday to me, then!

ADRIAN. *(Soothingly.)* Calm down, Dad. Calm down.

MEG. Is this it, then? This where we're eating?

MICKY. No. This isn't where we're eating, no. Not in here.

MEG. Going to say, they haven't even laid up, have they?

MICKY. *(Moving to the ballroom door.)* Where we're all going to be eating – is in here. *(Placing his hand on the doorknob.)* After you, my love!

> *(Opening the door, he waves her through.* **MEG** *steps into the darkened room.)*

MEG. *(As she does so.)* What? In here? In the dark? What are we doing eating in the pitch bloody –?

(The offstage room suddenly bursts into light and sound behind her. A great cheer. **MEG** *stands there in amazement, hand to her mouth for a moment.* **MICKY** *stands slightly behind and to one side of her.* **FAITH** *and* **ADRIAN** *stand back watching.* **MEG** *turns and dashes back into the room.* **MICKY**, *startled, turns and follows her back, closing the door as he does so.)*

MICKY. *(Alarmed.)* What's the matter? What the hell's the matter?

MEG. *(Breathlessly, fanning herself.)* Oh, my God! Oh, dear God!

ADRIAN. *(Equally alarmed.)* Mum? What's wrong?

FAITH. *(Likewise, with him.)* Meg, what's the matter?

MEG. I have to sit down. Sorry. I need to sit down, for a moment.

ADRIAN. *(Drawing up a chair.)* Yes, sit down.

FAITH. Sit down a minute.

MEG. *(Catching her breath.)* It was just the shock of seeing all those people. I'm so sorry.

ADRIAN. It was the shock, yes.

FAITH. The shock, yes. Must have been.

MEG. I'm sorry. I was just expecting us four. I'll be all right in a minute. Just get my breath. *(She takes one or two deep breaths.)*

FAITH. Do you need a glass of water? Adrian, fetch her a glass of water.

ADRIAN. Right. Where's the nearest –?

MICKY. Plenty to drink in there. Masses. They may even have water.

MEG. No, it's alright. I don't need water. Give me a minute, I'll be fine. *(She takes another couple of deep breaths.)*

MICKY. *(Only half joking.)* I hope you're not going to faint on me, are you? Be a shame to cancel. Cost a fortune that, lot in there.

MEG. Sorry, love, I didn't mean to spoil it for you. Sorry. *(She rises unsteadily.)*

FAITH. Careful.

ADRIAN. Easy, Mum.

MEG. I'm fine now, perfectly fine. *(To MICKY.)* Sorry, love. It's a wonderful surprise, thank you.

MICKY. Just enjoy yourself, that's all. Eat, drink and be merry. I mean to get my money's worth.

MEG. You arranged all this yourself, did you?

MICKY. 'course I did. Who else?

MEG. …only normally you leave things like this to me, don't you?

MICKY. *(Opening the door for her.)* In you go, face the music!

> *(A burst of lively chatter over the DJ's selection of vintage pop music*, which is now in full flow.)*

> *(MEG steps into the room, this time to a slightly milder reception from those who notice her re-arrival.)*

(Turning in the doorway.) You two coming in?

---

* A licence to produce BIRTHDAYS PAST, BIRTHDAYS PRESENT does not include a performance licence for any third-party or copyrighted music. Licensees should create an original composition or use music in the public domain. For further information, please see Music Use Note on page iii.

ADRIAN. *(With a glance at* **FAITH.***)* In a moment, Dad, could you give us a moment?

MICKY. Don't be too long. It's a good buffet. Don't miss it. Once this lot get stuck in...

> *(He closes the door, cutting off the sounds, which continue muted under.)*

ADRIAN. I think that took Mum's breath away, rather.

FAITH. Yes, poor thing, it must have done.

ADRIAN. But then I think those surprise things are always a bit hit and miss, aren't they? I mean, I think they're great fun if you're organising them but for the person concerned, they open the door and they probably see masses of people they never wanted to see again. People they thought they'd finally seen the back of years ago. Mind you, I don't think there's many of those in Mum's life. I think in general she's pleased to see everyone. I can't think of anyone. Even my Uncle Hal. I thought I saw him there.

FAITH. Oh, yes. Your uncle Hal. The black sheep, isn't he?

ADRIAN. Looks like he's brought someone with him. Another of his woman friends. Very colourful, she looked. Exotic. Foreign probably. He prefers foreign.

FAITH. I really admire your mother, you know –

ADRIAN. I know. You've said –

FAITH. I didn't really want to come this evening. I didn't think I was up to it –

ADRIAN. I know, you told me –

FAITH. – I didn't think I could face it all. But talking to your mother in there just now, it made me feel so much better. She's just such a positive person, isn't she? She's so calm and balanced and – I don't know – sane. I wish she'd been my real mother, you know. If I'd had her looking after me in those early days, perhaps I wouldn't have found things so – difficult. If I'd had Meg there for me instead of that woman who pretended to be my mother. On the rare occasions she could even remember she had a daughter. God. *(She shakes her head.)*

(A pause.)

(She sighs. She seems to have sunk into herself.)

*(**ADRIAN** seems used to it. He waits patiently.)*

By the way, I called the babysitter just now.

ADRIAN. Did you? What, again? Everything still alright, is it?

FAITH. They seem to be. So far. Colin was coughing again but they're both asleep now. He shouldn't be coughing, though, it's not natural.

ADRIAN. Well, he's got a cough, hasn't he? He's coughing because he's caught a cough. Kids are always catching coughs, aren't they? It's part of being a kid. When I was a kid, I was constantly coughing. I coughed most of my childhood away.

FAITH. *(Smiling faintly, shaking her head.)* You always try and make a joke of it, don't you? Why do you always do that?

ADRIAN. Well, I think it sometimes helps. Helps to see the brighter side, you know.

FAITH. *(With a little dry laugh.)* Brighter side? What brighter side, my darling, what brighter side are you referring to? *(Seriously.)* Adrian, perhaps we should talk. We really need to talk, don't we? Seriously?

ADRIAN. I don't think now is necessarily the best time to sit and talk, do you? I mean, it's my mother's –

(Before **ADRIAN** *can continue,* **MEG** *enters from the ballroom, glass in hand. A burst of loud music and chatter follow her.* She closes the door. She looks round for her handbag which she has left on a chair.)*

MEG. Oh, there it is! *(Brightly, slightly flushed from her first drink.)* He's done us proud! Your Dad's done us proud, bless him.

ADRIAN. Great. I'm glad, Mum.

MEG. I never thought he had it in him. I never thought he was capable of it. All these years, I totally misjudged him. You coming in then? Come on, join the party. Your Uncle Hal's doing this wild dance with this weird girl he's brought with him. Mariana, I think she's called. You coming?

ADRIAN. *(With a glance at* **FAITH.***)* In a moment.

FAITH. We won't be a moment.

MEG. *(Indicating her handbag.)* Well, keep an eye on that for me, will you? *(As she goes.)* Don't be long. You're missing all the fun! Fun! Fun! Fun!

*(***MEG** *goes out again, closing the door.)*

ADRIAN. Mum's having a good time, anyway.

FAITH. Yes. I'm glad she's happy. She deserves it.

ADRIAN. Uncle Hal appears to be enjoying himself, too, from the sound of it.

FAITH. I told your mother just now. That we were thinking of going for counselling.

---

* A licence to produce BIRTHDAYS PAST, BIRTHDAYS PRESENT does not include a performance licence for any third-party or copyrighted music. Licensees should create an original composition or use music in the public domain. For further information, please see Music Use Note on page iii.

ADRIAN. *(Slightly alarmed.)* Well, we sort of talked about it, yes. But I don't think we ever came to any firm decision, did we?

FAITH. It's been over two years, Adrian, and it's still not going right, is it? Things are still not right, are they?

ADRIAN. Most probably not, no. But I think we ought to –

FAITH. What do you mean, probably not? They're not right at all, are they, not at all?

ADRIAN. Listen, it's my Mum's birthday party, love, her sixtieth birthday. This is not a good time to start discussing our marriage, is it?

FAITH. Well, when then? When is it ever a good time?

ADRIAN. No, it's just with all this going on...

FAITH. I mean, we've been putting off talking about it for over a year now, Adrian...

ADRIAN. ...all those people in there...

FAITH. ...every time I bring it up, you try and change the subject. You never seem to want to talk about it, do you?

ADRIAN. ...my Dad's gone to all the trouble to...

FAITH. Do you?

ADRIAN. *(Giving in.)* Oh, what the hell, alright, come on then, let's talk. We'll talk, then.

(A slight pause.)

Come on, I'm listening.

FAITH. You want me to go first, then?

ADRIAN. Well, you might as well, you're the one who wants to talk.

FAITH. Alright. I've been very unhappy lately, you know that...

ADRIAN. Yes, I know you have. You keep telling me.

FAITH. The kids have noticed too. Christine certainly has. She said to me the other day, why are you so unhappy, Mummy?

ADRIAN. And what did you tell her?

FAITH. Nothing. I didn't tell her anything. I couldn't. I didn't know where to start.

ADRIAN. And when did you first get this feeling? Can you trace it back? To when you first felt it? To when you first felt it was all starting to go wrong?

FAITH. Well, if I'm being honest, it all started to go wrong for me the day we were married, really.

ADRIAN. *(Digesting this.)* Bloody hell! That far back? On our wedding day? You felt it all went wrong on our actual wedding day? What happened on our wedding day to depress you? Apart from your Mum being sick in the vestry, of course. But that can't have been the only reason, surely?

FAITH. Up till then it was so wonderful. Everything seemed so positive and – mended – somehow. Life had been broken in two and now it had been mended at last. I'd finally got over my first marriage and Matthew walking out on me and the kids. Abandoning us to go off with that woman. The shock of the divorce. That terrible feeling of emptiness. Loneliness. And then all of a sudden you came into my life and made it right again. As I say, it became so positive. We both fell in love, the kids seemed to like you, you were good with them. Yes, I know it did take a little time to start with, for both of us, you know, getting to know each other. It was so tentative to start with, wasn't it? We were almost shy with each other. But that was lovely. A sort of innocence. After being with him, Matthew. Which was anything but innocent, I can tell you. But, really and truly, I so looked forward to our wedding day when we could finally make us complete. Make us, you know, one. As it were.

ADRIAN. I see. You're not really talking about our wedding day, are you? You're actually talking about our wedding night, aren't you, if truth be told? That's when you felt it all went wrong, didn't you? Yes, I know we never quite managed it, not that particular night...

FAITH. I felt so rejected. As if you couldn't suddenly bear the sight of me. So unattractive.

ADRIAN. To be fair, there were two sides to it, love, be fair. In all honesty, half the time, I had the feeling there were three of us in there, in that bridal suite. You, me and him.

FAITH. Who?

ADRIAN. Your ex-husband. Matthew. He was practically there in bed with us, wasn't he? Metaphorically he was, anyway.

FAITH. Nonsense. I'd forgotten all about him by then.

ADRIAN. No, you hadn't! You hadn't at all, Faith. You may have thought you had but the bugger was still there with us the entire night. Every time I moved near you, tried to touch you, it was "no, not there! There! Matty always used to touch me there. That's where I like it."

FAITH. I never did that!

ADRIAN. You did, love. You probably weren't aware of it, but you kept on doing it all night. I felt I was taking some sort of bloody advanced driving test. Right hand down a bit! Now, straighten up! Straighten! I got so self-conscious and awkward, in the end your body literally dropped from my nerveless fingers. I know, he was a bastard, your ex-husband, and you were well shot of him. He treated you appallingly by the end and you probably wanted to put him out of your mind for ever. But you never forgot the sex, love. The sex lingered. It really did. Look, I don't, you know, want to sound falsely modest about it, but I reckon he was a league above me in the sex department. I was never going to match that.

FAITH. You know what your Dad said to me on our wedding day? At the reception?

ADRIAN. Oh, no, don't tell me –

FAITH. He was slightly drunk but not that much, he leant over and whispered, "Take my tip, once he gets you into bed, love, you'd do well to brace yourself!"

ADRIAN. *(Unhappily.)* I don't know where Dad gets these ideas from, I really don't.

FAITH. *(Gently.)* Oh, I'm sorry. I'm so sorry. I thought it was me.

ADRIAN. It wasn't you. Not at all. It was your bloody first husband.

> *(She kisses him gently on the mouth. He appears to be about to respond when* **MICKY** *enters from the ballroom, carrying a drink. He appears hot and slightly drunk. The background behind him has grown noticeably louder.)*

MICKY. Whey-hey! The joint is definitely jumping –

> *(He breaks off, realising he is interrupting something, as the others break apart.)*

Oh, I do beg your pardon! Carry on. Don't mind me. Hey, that exotic bit of your Uncle Hal's, Mariana. She's a bit tasty. Promised me the next dance. Reckon I'm in there with a chance! Your mother's well away. I tell you, it's like a bloody kids' disco in there! Come on, you two. Give her a night off for once, lad, she's earned it!

(He goes out again, closing the door.)

ADRIAN. Alright, listen. Like you said, let's be positive. Let's look on the bri – Let's just stop a moment and count our blessings, shall we? Number one. We've got each other, right? We've got a roof over our heads. I've got a good well-paid job. You've got a good job, too, waiting for you when you go back. Soon as you feel up to it again. You've got a couple of lovely kids, both in good working order. Admittedly one's got a cough, but that'll soon pass. So, let's concentrate on all the good things we've got in our lives for a change, all the good things we've got to be... *(He breaks off.)*

*(**FAITH** is now crying.)*

(Mildly exasperated.) What's the matter now, for God's sake, what the hell are you crying for now?

FAITH. *(With a wail.)* I'm thinking of the people who've got nothing at all!

ADRIAN. Oh, bloody hell! *(Pulling her to him and holding her tightly.)* Come on then, easy... Easy now...

FAITH. *(Muffled.)* I'm sorry. I'm sorry...

ADRIAN. *(Soothingly, stroking her hair.)* It's alright, alright... Take your time, take your time, now...

FAITH. *(Tearfully.)* Don't say that...

ADRIAN. What?

FAITH. "Take your time". That's what they always say to disabled people, "take your time".

ADRIAN. *(At a complete loss.)* Oh, hell...

(He continues to hold her, looking to the heavens as if for support.)

(**MEG** *enters from the ballroom, hot, breathless and somewhat dishevelled.*)

(*She makes straight for her handbag and helps herself to a tissue.*)

MEG. (*As she does so.*) If that woman doesn't keep her thieving little hands off my husband, I'm going to wring her neck, in a minute...

(**MEG** *goes out again, closing the door.*)

ADRIAN. I think the kids haven't quite forgotten Matthew, either. Whenever little Colin falls down and hurts himself, if I pick him up, he says, no, I want my daddy, I want my daddy! Christine said the other day, you can't have your daddy, Colin, Daddy's not ever coming back. Gran says we have to make do with Adrian.

(*They sit for a moment.*)

FAITH. We need to think about it seriously though, Adrian. Counselling? Don't we?

ADRIAN. What sort of counselling?

FAITH. Marriage counselling. Sex counselling. I've heard about this very marvellous woman, she helped –

ADRIAN. Oh, no! Then we'll have someone else in bed with us, won't we? Don't touch this bit, touch that bit! Left hand down a bit! Never get any sleep, will we?

FAITH. No, seriously, Adrian. I mean it

ADRIAN. I don't know why things always have to be so complicated, I really don't.

FAITH. Because life is complicated, Adrian, it's terribly complicated. Just being alive, day-to-day, it's complicated.

ADRIAN. I'm saying, it doesn't need to be though, does it? I mean, it should all be fun, shouldn't it? Like Mum said just now, fun, fun, fun!

FAITH. Adrian, life is not a joking matter, it really isn't…

(Before she can continue, they are interrupted by a loud crash from the ballroom. Even through the closed door, the sound of screams and the prolonged clatter of breaking crockery.)

*(**ADRIAN** springs to his feet. **FAITH** looks alarmed.)*

ADRIAN. What the hell's that?

*(Before he can move further, the ballroom door bursts open and **MICKY** enters in a hurry. From behind him, a fair amount of pandemonium.)*

MICKY. *(Breathlessly.)* Adrian, lad, come and help me with your mother! Quickly! Help me!

ADRIAN. *(Moving to the door.)* What's happened? Is she alright? Is Mum alright?

MICKY. *(As he goes.)* She's alright. I don't know about the other one, though…

ADRIAN. *(Following him, seeing the scene beyond.)* Oh, my God! What the hell happened…?

*(They both go out, leaving the door open. **FAITH** moves to the doorway to witness the scene.)*

MICKY. *(Off, above the din.)* …now break it up, do you hear? Break it up, you two!

*(In a moment, a bedraggled **MEG** is brought in backwards, dragged by **MICKY** and **ADRIAN**)*

holding her arms. She is still flailing and struggling, having apparently been lifted off her opponent.)

MEG. *(As she is brought on, beside herself with fury.)* ...I'll kill her... I'll kill the silly little bitch... I'll kill her...

MICKY. Now, calm down! Just calm down! Get a hold of yourself, woman! You're a bloody disgrace, on your birthday! No way to behave on your birthday, fighting over me. I'm not worth fighting over, am I?

MEG. *(Wrenching herself free of them and wheeling on them both, angrily.)* No, you bastard, you're certainly not! You're certainly not worth fighting over, you pathetic... Look at you! Just look at you! Pathetic excuse for a man! Sixty-five years old and you still go weak at the knees at the sight of a couple of silicone tits, don't you? Pathetic! Fucking men! All of you! I've had it up to here with you!

*(**FAITH** stands open-mouthed, stunned by this outburst. During the last, **MICKY** has closed the ballroom door.)*

*(**ADRIAN** is aware of the effect this has had on his wife.)*

ADRIAN. *(Alarmed but trying to keep things calm.)* Mum! Come on, Mum. Pull yourself together, you've had too much to drink now, haven't you?

MEG. *(Turning on him.)* As for you, you're as bad as him! You're as bad as he is! Look what you're doing to her! She's desperate, poor love! Hardly knows what day it is, does she? Well, never mind, Faith, darling, never mind, my love! You and me, we'll sort the buggers out between us, won't we? Never you mind, darling, we'll sort 'em out, won't we...?

> (**FAITH** *has had quite enough and runs out of the room.*)

(*Puzzled.*) Where's she gone? Where the hell'd she go? (*To* **ADRIAN**.) Where'd she go, then, your little wife?

ADRIAN. (*Rather lamely.*) I think she suddenly remembered the babysitter.

MEG. Oh. Babysitter. (*She sits.*)

MICKY. (*Inwardly rather shaken.*) I'd better go and see to things out here. They must have broken about fifty quid's worth of crockery between them. (*Fiercely to* **MEG**.) Sixty years old. Be ashamed of yourself. Adrian, speak to your mother! Talk some sense into her!

> (*He goes out.*)
>
> (*A silence.*)
>
> (**ADRIAN** *stands unhappily.* **MEG** *recovers.*)

ADRIAN. (*At last.*) I really don't know what to say to you, Mum. I really don't.

MEG. It's never easy, darling. It never gets any easier. We've been at it now for over forty years, your Dad and me, and it never gets bloody easier. I don't think we're none of us meant to live together for any length of time. Be careful of that one, love, be careful, she's brought a load of baggage with her and she'll cause you sadness. You know what I'm saying?

> (**ADRIAN** *considers this for a moment.*)

ADRIAN. Yes, I do. I know exactly what you're saying, Mum. But all the same, I'll give it a go.

MEG. Thought you would. Never listen to your mother, do you? Well, don't listen to your batty father, either.

ADRIAN. She'll be waiting for me to drive her home. Alright now, are you?

MEG. I'm alright.

ADRIAN. Sure?

> (**MEG** *nods.*)

Right. See you later. Happy birthday again.

> (*He goes out.*)

MEG. *(Calling after him.)* Don't say I didn't warn you! *(To herself.)* Bloody kids. Never listen to you, do they? Oh, Adrian, dear little Adrian, I don't know what's going to become of you, I'm sure.

> (*As she sits there waiting for her husband to return, the lights fade to:*)
>
> (*Blackout.*)

End of Act I

ACT II

Scene one

(**ADRIAN**'s *thirtieth. Twenty-five years ago. The living room of* **ADRIAN**'s *flat. It is of modest size but surprisingly tidy for a bachelor apartment. Three entrances. The front door, leading from the outside hallway directly into the room. The second, a curtained archway into to a small kitchenette. The third, leading to bedroom and bathroom. This main room is sparsely furnished with a sofa, armchair, coffee table and a bare sideboard on which sits a modestly priced music centre. On the coffee table is a small brown paper parcel which has apparently arrived through the post. In a moment,* **ADRIAN** *enters from the bedroom. Although it is already mid-morning, being a Saturday and his birthday, he has only just showered, is barefoot and pulling on his jumper over his shirt. He stops at the music centre and presses a couple of buttons. A soft classical music CD plays.** *He hums along contentedly. He sits on the sofa and contemplates the parcel on the table. He examines it.)*

---

* A licence to produce BIRTHDAYS PAST, BIRTHDAYS PRESENT does not include a performance licence for any third-party or copyrighted music. Licensees should create an original composition or use music in the public domain. For further information, please see Music Use Note on page iii.

ADRIAN. *(Reading.)* "Not to be opened till the twenty-fourth." Oh, I know who this'll be from. You never forget, do you, Gran, bless your heart?

> *(He removes the outer string and brown paper wrapping. Within this lies a gift-wrapped package together with an attached card in an envelope.)*

> *(He removes the card. It has a brightly coloured, cheerful design but is clearly intended for someone at least twenty years younger.)*

(Reading.) "Happy birthday, dearest boy,

May this day be filled with joy,

Gifts galore and scrumptious cake,

It's your day, for goodness sake!"

(Shaking his head.) Thank you, Gran. It's the thought that counts. What have you bought me this year, then?

> *(He removes the wrapping paper. It contains a children's game.)*

(Reading the box lid.) "Farmyard Snap. Suitable from thirty-six-months upward." Not again! I'm thirty, Gran, I'm thirty-years-old, for God's sake! *(Reflecting.)* Thirty. God, I'm thirty. Where did the time go? I'm old. Decrepit! *(Returning to the game.)* Farmyard Snap. Thanks very much, Gran, I'll have fun playing this on my own, won't I? Well, it makes a change from Animal Snap, I suppose. Or Jungle Snap. Or Crocodile Snap. Every bloody year. I'm snapped out, Gran. *(Pushing the box aside.)* Ah, well, another one for the jumble sale.

> *(He rises and takes the card to the empty sideboard.)*

Here you go. You can sit here with all the others, can't you? I think there'll be room. Alongside the card my loving sister forgot to send me from Dubai. Thank you so much, Sonia.

(He places the card in solitary state.)

There! Lovely. Not too crowded for you, is it? *(With another wave of depression.)* Thirty! Bloody hell, thirty!

(He does an exaggeratedly elderly walk to the kitchenette.)

(Before he can get there, the doorbell rings.)

Who the hell –? *(Moving to the door.)* It'll be the postman weighed down with gifts, poor bugger. Hardly able to get up the stairs with so many – *(Opening the door.)* Oh.

(Standing there clutching a gift-wrapped parcel is **CHARITY**, *an attractive girl in her mid-twenties.)*

CHARITY. *(Cheerfully.)* Hi! Adrian? Are you Adrian?

ADRIAN. Yes. I'm Adrian.

CHARITY. Happy birthday, darlin'! Brought you a present.

ADRIAN. A present? For me?

CHARITY. From your uncle. Your Uncle Henry.

ADRIAN. *(Mystified.)* My Uncle Henry? I don't have an uncle – Oh, you mean, Uncle Hal? My Uncle Hal?

CHARITY. Whatever. Can I come in?

ADRIAN. *(Stepping aside, warily.)* Yes, I suppose so. Sure.

*(***CHARITY** *steps inside.)*

> *(He watches her suspiciously but closes the front door, checking the hallway as he does so.)*

(Moving back into the room.) How did you get up here, then? Who let you in the front door?

CHARITY. Oh, a man. Bloke walking his dog let me in.

ADRIAN. *(Frowning.)* He shouldn't have done that. They're always doing that in this building. Just let anyone in.

CHARITY. Ah, but I'm not just anyone, am I? I'm from your uncle Henry, aren't I?

ADRIAN. Hal. Uncle Hal.

CHARITY. Whatever.

ADRIAN. Yes, but the bloke with the dog wasn't to know that, was he? So far as he was concerned, you could have been anyone.

CHARITY. *(Slightly sharper.)* No, but I'm not just anyone, am I? I'm me. Listen, do you want to stand here arguing on your birthday or do you want your present? Because I'm easy either way, darlin'. I can just as easy leave again. Now, do you want your soddin' present, or not?

ADRIAN. Yes, alright.

CHARITY. *(Prompting.)* Please.

ADRIAN. Please. *(Indicating the package.)* Is that it, then?

CHARITY. Yeah. Part of it. Here.

> *(**CHARITY** hands him the gift. He takes it.)*

(Prompting again.) Thank you.

ADRIAN. Thanks.

> *(He stands holding the gift as if waiting for her to leave. She waits.)*

CHARITY. Aren't you going to open it, then?

ADRIAN. What?

CHARITY. Go on, open it.

ADRIAN. *(Somewhat reluctantly.)* Yes. Alright.

> *(He removes the wrapping. It is a boxed, expensive bottle of vodka with a gift label attached.)*

Ah. Vodka.

CHARITY. Nice. It's a good one, that.

ADRIAN. Is it?

CHARITY. You could get proper rat arsed on that.

ADRIAN. I don't drink.

CHARITY. Don't you?

ADRIAN. He knows that. I never touch the stuff.

CHARITY. Vodka?

ADRIAN. Alcohol. I don't drink at all. Never have done.

CHARITY. Oh. That's a shame. Bit of a waste then, isn't it?

ADRIAN. *(Putting the bottle on the table.)* Yes. It is. You said this is part of the present?

CHARITY. Right.

ADRIAN. Where's the other part, then?

CHARITY. Here.

> *(She lets her coat fall away. She is standing in her high heels and underwear.)*

ADRIAN. Jesus!

CHARITY. I'm the other part, darlin'. Courtesy of your Uncle Henry. Two hours of free fun and frolic, whatever you fancy.

ADRIAN. *(Stunned.)* Two hours?

CHARITY. That's upfront, that's prepaid. If you want extra time, you pay for it yourself. But you won't need that, I guarantee. We can get through a lot in two hours, I promise. You won't be disappointed.

ADRIAN. *(Incredulously.)* He's paid you for two hours? To be with me? To spend two hours with me?

CHARITY. Brighten up your birthday, won't it?

ADRIAN. Sex? Are you talking about sex?

CHARITY. Well, I'm not here to play fucking table tennis, darlin'. Not dressed like this, I'm not.

ADRIAN. *(Agitatedly, shaking his head.)* Oh, my God, no, no, no!

> *(He paces around distressed. She watches him.)*

(Finally.) No!

CHARITY. Don't tell me you don't do that neither? Sex? You're not into sex, neither?

ADRIAN. Not like this, no. Not paying for it, no, certainly not!

CHARITY. Well, you're not paying, are you? He's the one who's paying, Uncle Henry. He's the one forked out. Far as you're concerned it's a freebie.

ADRIAN. That's beside the point. It's the principle. Paying for sex. It's totally unethical. What was he thinking of? Paying for me to have sex with someone I don't even know! A complete stranger? What does he take me for?

CHARITY. Look, I'm perfectly clean, darling, if that's what's worrying you. I have regular checks.

ADRIAN. *(Firmly.)* No, sorry, I want no part of this, do you hear? Will you please leave now. Just put your coat on again and leave. Please! Kindly leave!

(A slight pause.)

(Then she picks up her coat and puts it on again.)

CHARITY. *(As she does so.)* Right-o. No skin off my nose, is it? All the same to me, darlin'. Makes no difference to me. Happy birthday and fuck you!

(She starts to move to the door.)

ADRIAN. *(Picking up the bottle.)* Yes, and you can take this stuff with you, as well.

(He hands her back the bottle.)

CHARITY. *(Coolly.)* Thanks, I'll need it. He might have warned me you're a bloody Jehovah's Witness. Christ, what a waste of a bloody day, eh? After I lugged all the way out here, too!

(She stands with her hand on the door handle, her head resting wearily against the door.)

ADRIAN. *(Suddenly feeling rather guilty.)* Look, I'm sorry. I didn't mean to sound... I mean, it's nothing...personal you know. I'm sorry, turning you away like this... I mean, on the one hand, you're obviously perfectly happy to do this sort of thing for money, whereas, on the other hand –

CHARITY. No, I'm not that happy with it either, darlin', not at all. Don't think for a minute I'm happy. It's just some of us, we don't have the fucking choice, do we?

ADRIAN. No, it's just that I – I feel terrible about – rejecting you like this –

CHARITY. It's not a problem, I've said, it's not a problem, darlin' …

ADRIAN. *(Awkwardly.)* No, you're really attractive. You've got a most wonderful body, you know. Really most, most –

CHARITY. Don't dig it any deeper, darlin', you're deep enough already. You're up to your nose in it, leave it. Just leave it out. If you go on any more, I swear I'll club you round the head with this bottle, alright? And that would be a waste of good vodka. So, ta-ra. Nice to have known you. Or not to have known you. Bye-bye, hope we won't meet again sometime. *(She opens the door to leave.)*

ADRIAN. Listen, don't go quite yet. Stay for a minute, please. Please.

CHARITY. *(Hesitating.)* Why? What's there to stay for?

ADRIAN. We could – you know – have a chat, couldn't we? A cup of tea perhaps?

CHARITY. *(Dubiously.)* A cup of tea?

ADRIAN. Well, you know. Anything. Look, you've already been paid for it, haven't you? So, you might as well, mightn't you? You know, stay? Get my two hours' worth, anyway.

CHARITY. *(Guardedly.)* I don't mind chatting, if you prefer that. A lot of people prefer to chat. Well, I say chat. Mostly they talk about themselves, I just nod occasionally, you know, as if I'm listening. Which I'm not. Because I've usually heard it all before, most of it. But if you want to chat, that's fine by me. Not sure about the tea, though. If you don't mind, I think I'll have a glass of this.

ADRIAN. *(Rather pleased.)* Great. I'll fetch you a glass. Sit down, please.

(He goes briefly into the kitchenette.)

(She sits and removes the bottle from its box, which she tosses onto the sofa.)

(Offstage.) I'll do my best not to talk about myself too much, I promise.

CHARITY. As I say, don't worry, I'll have heard it before. There's nothing original under the sun, darlin'. It may be new to you, I promise you, it won't be to me.

ADRIAN. *(Off, laughing.)* I must say that does make us all sound boringly the same.

CHARITY. *(Dryly.)* Yes, and?

ADRIAN. *(Returning with two glasses.)* Why don't we be totally original and talk about you for a change?

CHARITY. Me?

ADRIAN. Why not?

CHARITY. We're certainly not talking about me, darlin'. No way are we talking about me. That's strictly off-limits, that is.

ADRIAN. Why's that?

CHARITY. Christ, I'm not being paid enough for that. Oh, two glasses, I see?

ADRIAN. I thought I'd have a sip. Keep you company. If I may?

CHARITY. *(Shrugging.)* It's your present.

(She pours two glasses of vodka. A large one for her, a slightly smaller one for him.)

*(Meantime, **ADRIAN** clears the vodka box from the sofa. He looks at the gift label attached.)*

ADRIAN. My God.

CHARITY. What?

ADRIAN. *(Reading.)* "Have a great birthday, old lad. Give her one from me, love from Uncle Hal."

CHARITY. *(Dryly.)* He always had a sense of humour, Henry.

ADRIAN. Have you known him long?

CHARITY. Long enough. *(Raising her glass.)* Cheers, then. Happy birthday.

ADRIAN. Cheers! *(Taking a sip.)* Oh, God!

CHARITY. Good, isn't it?

ADRIAN. *(His eyes watering slightly.)* Strong.

(A pause.)

Well.

CHARITY. So, what are we going to talk about? You promised not to talk about you and I refuse to talk about me, so what else is there?

ADRIAN. Well. Politics?

CHARITY. Boring.

ADRIAN. Religion?

CHARITY. Forget that.

ADRIAN. Sex, then. You know, sex in theory. Theoretical sex.

CHARITY. What the fuck's theoretical sex? There's no such thing. You're either doing it or you're not.

(Another pause.)

What do you do for a living, then? If I may be permitted to ask?

ADRIAN. I work for Dunstan's. In the accounts department.

CHARITY. Oh, you're an accountant, are you?

ADRIAN. No, I just work in the accounts department. I'm not an accountant.

CHARITY. Oh, I see. *(She doesn't.)*

(Slight pause.)

ADRIAN. I won't ask you what you do.

CHARITY. *(Sourly.)* I work for social services.

(Another pause.)

Jesus, this is fun, isn't it? Enjoying your birthday, are you? What time you due back in the monastery?

(Another slight pause.)

(Indicating the children's game.) What's that, then? What's all that there?

ADRIAN. Oh, that's from my grandmother. I used to play snap with her for hours, when I was a kid. I used to go and stay with her. Ever since, every single birthday she insists on sending me these games. As though I were still ten. In fact, she probably thinks I am still ten. Usually it's games like that, you know. Games of snap. Variations of snap, anyway.

CHARITY. Oh, yes, snap. We used to play that all the time.

ADRIAN. What, when you were a kid?

CHARITY. When I was in youth custody. It was the only game they let us play that didn't involve money. What's this one about, then? Farm Snap?

ADRIAN. I think it involves animals, probably. Farm animals.

CHARITY. Farm animals?

ADRIAN. As opposed to Kings and Queens and Jacks and so on. It's a variant on animal snap. You ever play animal snap, did you?

CHARITY. Not in prison. Be a bit dangerous. Might have given one or two of them ideas. 'Specially the big girls.

ADRIAN. I used to play it quite a bit with Gran. She was an absolute demon. Lightning reflexes, even at that age. *(A sudden idea.)* Tell you what, fancy a game, do you?

CHARITY. After I've had another glass of this, I might. You want a drop more?

ADRIAN. Yes, just a drop. You get used to it after a bit, don't you? Sort of grows on you, doesn't it? *(Opening the game, briefly glancing at the contents.)* Yes, right. *(Tossing the instructions aside.)* Ignore those. No time for official rules. We'll play according to Gran's rules, shall we? *(Dividing the cards in half.)* You take those, I'll have these. You need two matching animals and whenever you see two of them matching, you have to make the noise of the animal, you see? But if you make the wrong noise, instead of having a snap pool, you have to do the forfeit.

CHARITY. Forfeit? What sort of forfeit?

ADRIAN. The person has to impersonate the animal, you see? Like, if it was a monkey, say, you need to go like this. *(He demonstrates.)* Only there won't be any monkeys, of course, because it's farm animals.

CHARITY. *(Doubtfully.)* I'm not at all sure about this...

ADRIAN. Come on, you ready?

CHARITY. *(Taking another swig.)* Hang on. Right. Ready.

(Both sit poised ready with their respective packs of cards.)

ADRIAN. And, go!

*(Simultaneously they put down their top cards in front of them. Then a second. Then a third. The tension mounts. Then a fourth, at which point **ADRIAN** makes a bleating sound.)*

CHARITY. What was that?

ADRIAN. Sheep. Two sheep.

CHARITY. Oh, yes. That's a sheep noise, is it?

*(**ADRIAN** picks up the cards and puts them with his own deck.)*

ADRIAN. *(As he does so.)* More or less. Right. Here we go again.

*(They start to deal again. Another two cards dealt and on the third, **CHARITY** makes a sudden chicken-like squawk which she rapidly stifles.)*

CHARITY. Oh, no. Sorry.

ADRIAN. That's a chicken. My one's turkey. You have to do the forfeit. You have to do your chicken.

CHARITY. Oh, shit! *(Removing her coat.)* Hang on, I'm getting hot. Right. Here comes my chicken.

*(She does her chicken impersonation which in her semi-naked state is quite erotic, including a lot of wriggling of her rear end close to **ADRIAN**'s face. He looks discreetly away.)*

There you are. I've done my chicken. That's your lot. You know, I don't recognise half these bloody animals, not when they got feathers on. Are they all off the farm then, are they?

ADRIAN. Yes, most of them. Have you never been on a farm?

CHARITY. No. Never.

ADRIAN. Never been to the country?

CHARITY. Nearest I've been is Golders Green.

ADRIAN. *(A little shocked.)* God!

CHARITY. One of my regulars lives out there. Nice old Jewish gentleman. Real gent. Inner city girl, me. *(Taking another swig.)* Right, here we go again.

> *(Another round.)*
>
> *(Already the alcohol is beginning to take effect, particularly on **ADRIAN**.)*
>
> *(Another couple of cards are dealt.)*
>
> *(On the third, he "hee-haws" triumphantly.)*

ADRIAN. Two donkeys! Two donkeys!

CHARITY. Oh, fuck it! I could see they were matching. I just didn't know what soddin' noise they made, did I? I thought those was horses.

> **(ADRIAN** *gathers up the dealt cards again.)*

(Gazing at him with curiosity.) When did you last have it, then?

ADRIAN. What?

CHARITY. Sex? When did you last have sex? Do you mind me asking?

ADRIAN. Yes, I certainly do mind you asking. Nothing to do with you.

CHARITY. Only I'm curious, that's all. My feeling is – only I've got an instinct for these things – my instinct is you've never ever had it, have you?

ADRIAN. *(Indignantly.)* I most certainly have. I don't know why you should think that. I've had it. I've frequently had it.

CHARITY. When's the last time? Can you remember? The last time you had it?

ADRIAN. Yes, I remember very clearly. If you must know, it was with a girl, a friend of my sister's as a matter of fact.

CHARITY. Where? Where did you have it?

ADRIAN. In my bedroom. *(After a slight pause.)* Or, more precisely, in my bedroom cupboard. As it happens.

CHARITY. *(Blankly.)* In your cupboard?

ADRIAN. Yes. With someone I cannot name.

CHARITY. You prefer it in cupboards, do you?

ADRIAN. God no, nothing like that?

CHARITY. Got a thing about cupboards, have you?

ADRIAN. No, not at all.

CHARITY. This friend of your sister's, she likes it in cupboards then, does she?

ADRIAN. No, we both happened to find ourselves in a cupboard together and we both – suddenly felt like it and – that's all.

CHARITY. Well, I have to say, you're very kinky. For an accountant.

ADRIAN. A bookkeeper. I'm technically a bookkeeper.

CHARITY. And when was the very first time you had it, can you remember that?

ADRIAN. Yes, I can. *(He hesitates.)* It was with a friend of my sister's, in a cupboard.

CHARITY. What, another cupboard?

ADRIAN. *(Coming clean.)* No, it was the same cupboard. It was exactly the same occasion, actually. Thirteen years ago. My sister's birthday party.

CHARITY. Thirteen years?

ADRIAN. Yes.

CHARITY. Nothing since then?

ADRIAN. Just been waiting – you know – for the right person. To come along. You know.

CHARITY. *(Slightly awed.)* Thirteen years. She'll have a lot coming her way, won't she? Lucky girl, eh?

ADRIAN. Look, can we get on with the game now, please. *(Preparing to deal again.)* Ready?

> *(They deal again. This time two cards go through, before:)*

CHARITY. *(Triumphantly.)* Moo! Moo! Moo! Two cows!

> **(ADRIAN** *looks doubtful.)*

It is! Two cows! It is!

ADRIAN. Yours is a cow.

CHARITY. So's yours. Yours is a cow, as well.

ADRIAN. No, mine's a bull. My one's a bull.

CHARITY. *(Scrutinising her card.)* Is it? You sure? Not much of a bull, is he? He ain't got much tackle, has he?

ADRIAN. Well, it's a kid's game, it's meant for kids.

CHARITY. They'll have to find out sooner or later, won't they? I wish I'd seen a bull first, before I came across the real thing. How can you tell that's a bull?

ADRIAN. He's got a ring through his nose.

CHARITY. Oh, I do beg his pardon, I'm sure. Here's me, all these years, looking at the wrong end, silly me!

ADRIAN. Now you have to do your cow.

CHARITY. What?

ADRIAN. Now, you do your cow. Go on.

CHARITY. What, again? Oh, sod it! I'm sick of this, I'm doing all the animals, aren't I? When are you going to do an animal? When's it your turn?

ADRIAN. When I lose, that's when I do one.

CHARITY. *(Pouring herself another glass.)* Well, I'm not doing any more after this. Right. One cow coming up – I've never even met a bloody cow. Except hanging up in a butcher's shop.

> *(She does a rather cursory half-hearted cow impression.)*

Moo! Moo! There! Good enough for you?

ADRIAN. *(Beginning to have trouble with his speech.)* More like a hippo. Hippo. Pot. Muss. Pardon.

CHARITY. Well, that's my last one. I'm not doing any more.

ADRIAN. You want to stop then?

CHARITY. No, I don't want to stop, only just got started, haven't we? Tell you what, though, we're changing the rules. Sod your grandma. Let's do a strip version, shall we? Animal strip snap. Every time you get a forfeit you have to take something off.

ADRIAN. What, an item of clo'ing, you mean? Oh, come on...

CHARITY. You've got a head start on me, haven't you? You got more clothes on.

ADRIAN. *(Really starting to slur his speech now.)* That's completely and utt'ly 'diculous! 'solutely 'diculous!

CHARITY. *(Also starting to lose coherence.)* Come on then! Here go. Animal Snip strap – slip slap... Christ, I can't even say it! We're both uttly pissed, aren't we? This stuff must be a hunnerd percent lee ful. Hunnerd percent al hol. My bloody mow's not whirring proper. Come on! Come on then! Here go then! Offwigo!

> *(They start to put down cards rather haphazardly.)*
>
> *(**ADRIAN**, after a couple of cards, makes a curious whistling noise.)*

Whasssat? Whassat menbe?

ADRIAN. 'srabbit Two rabbits. Got two rabbits.

CHARITY. 'notarabbit. Thassafuckincat! Thassafuckincat, tharris! Even I know thassafuckincat!

ADRIAN. God! Sotis! Issafuckincat!

CHARITY. *(Triumphantly.)* Off! Off! Off! Gerremoff, then!

> *(**ADRIAN** rises, trying to maintain his dignity.)*

ADRIAN. I 'fuse. I 'fuse to take off my trussers! I res'lutely 'fuse!

CHARITY. *(Aggressively.)* Gerremoff! You bugger!

ADRIAN. *(With dignity.)* I 'tend to 'move, my – joolly wumper!

CHARITY. Whasssat? Your joolly wumper! Wasafucksa joolly wumper!

ADRIAN. *(Carefully enunciating.)* My woolly jumper. 'taking this off'stead.

> *(He removes his sweater.)*

CHARITY. *(As he does so.)* Whey-hey! Thissessiting! 'slike being with the Chippendles… Chipplendles… Chipples…

(**ADRIAN** *sits down again, only this time beside her on the sofa.*)

ADRIAN. Play on! Plon!

(*They start to play further cards with even more inaccuracy.*)

CHARITY. (*Suddenly excitedly.*) Meow! Meow? It's a pussy. There's a pussy!

ADRIAN. That's not a pussy.

CHARITY. How would you know?

ADRIAN. No way is that a pussy. It's a rabbit. Defin'tely a rabbit, this time! Now, take something off. Your turn to take something off.

CHARITY. Thassapity! I could have done my pussy for you. I could have given my pussy.

(*She swings her legs up onto his lap.*)

Thereyarr! Gerremoff, then! You takemoff!

ADRIAN. (*Momentarily nonplussed, comprehending.*) Oh, right! Rightchar!

(*With difficulty, he starts to unfasten her suspenders.*)

Fiddly, aren't they? Fiddly fings...

CHARITY. (*Staring up at him.*) You know you're a very sexy man. 'Streemly sexy.

ADRIAN. Thanks very much.

CHARITY. 'Streemly sexy. For an accountant.

ADRIAN. No, I keep telling you, I'm not an accountant. No way am I an accountant. I'm a bookkeeper. A bookkeeper. I keep books.

CHARITY. *(Wriggling slightly in his lap.)* A bookkeeper, eh? I think I can feel where you keep it, big boy!

ADRIAN. *(Still struggling with her fastenings.)* Oh, effing fiddlesticks!

> (**CHARITY** *swings herself back onto the floor and rises.*)

CHARITY. Come on, then! Come on, you bugger!

ADRIAN. What are you doing? Where we going?

> *(She starts to pull him towards the bedroom with one hand, whilst unfastening his trousers with the other.)*

CHARITY. *(As she does so.)* We're gonna find a cupboard! Get these off you and we'll find a nice cosy cupboard...

ADRIAN. *(Now well up for it.)* Oh, good! There's one along here. There's a lovely cupboard along here...

CHARITY. ...let's go, let's go, baby...

ADRIAN. ...there's the airing cupboard, nice and warm...

CHARITY. ...nice and warm... God, I'm hot enough already...

> *(They have nearly made it to the doorway when the front door bell rings loudly. They freeze.)*

Whassat? Whatthefuckwassat?

> *(It rings again. Then, from the landing outside, we hear the voices of* **MEG** *and* **MICKY** *singing* **"HAPPY BIRTHDAY".*)

ADRIAN. Oh, my God, it's my parents! It's my bloody parents! They can't find you here, they can't see all this!

> *(They both scramble about, gathering up things. Both have miraculously sobered up.*

She randomly gathers up items including her shoes and his sweater but fails to locate her coat which **ADRIAN**, *in his frenzy, has picked up and tossed into the kitchen.)*

CHARITY. *(As they do so.)* Why didn't you say your soddin' parents were coming?

ADRIAN. I didn't know they were coming, did I? It's a birthday surprise! I might have guessed it! Quickly! Quickly! Wait in here!

(He bundles her towards the bedroom.)

CHARITY. *(As he does so.)* Where's my coat? What have you done with my bloody coat, for God's sake?

(He pushes her through the doorway and they both momentarily vanish from sight. The offstage bedroom door slams.)

*(***ADRIAN** *returns and scuttles round doing his best to tidy away the game. He also hides the depleted bottle and glasses in the kitchen. Offstage, the singing ceases.)*

MICKY. *(Off, calling.)* Adrian! Adrian? Are you there, son?

MEG. *(Off, calling.)* It's only us, love! Your mum and dad! We've come to wish you a happy birthday, darling!

MICKY. *(Off, calling.)* Happy birthday, son! Come to wish you happy birthday!

(The doorbell rings again.)

ADRIAN. *(Giving up on his efforts.)* Oh, hell!

(He moves to the front door and opens it. **MEG** *and* **MICKY** *are waiting there. She is fifty, he is fifty-five. Both of them carry birthday gifts.)*

MICKY. Surprise!

MEG. Surprise!

ADRIAN. Mum! Lovely to see you!

MICKY. *(As they enter.)* Happy birthday, son!

MEG. Happy birthday, love!

ADRIAN. Sorry, I wasn't expecting you. The place is a bit of a mess, I'm afraid.

MEG. *(Surveying the scene.)* Oh, my goodness, yes, see what you mean. What have you been doing?

ADRIAN. Grandma sent me one of her games for my birthday.

MEG. Oh, she's wonderful, isn't she? Never forgets, does she?

MICKY. Never forgets. Remarkable at her age…

ADRIAN. I've just been having a go at it, you know. On my own. Trying it out.

MICKY. *(Reading the box lid.)* Farmyard Snap. That's the same as ordinary snap, is it?

ADRIAN. Yeah. Only with farm animals…

MEG. Snap? You'd have a job playing snap on your own, wouldn't you?

ADRIAN. Yes, it was quite tricky, yes. *(Laughing.)* Had to keep my eyes closed, most of the time.

MEG. Oh, it's so sad, isn't it, Micky? I hate to think of you sitting here playing snap all on your own, on your birthday. We're sorry not to have come earlier, but your Dad had a late shift last night.

MICKY. Coach party. Back to Rotherham from Brussels. Didn't get in till the small hours. Trouble at the ferry.

MEG. As usual.

ADRIAN. Oh, dear.

MEG. Now, sit down, both of you. I'll put the kettle on. You could do with a cuppa, Micky, couldn't you?

MICKY. Wouldn't say no.

(**ADRIAN** *attempts to continue tidying.*)

MEG. No, I'll do that, Adrian, don't you bother.

ADRIAN. It's all right, I'll...

MEG. No, not on your birthday. I'll do it. You sit down, have a chat with your Dad. We've brought your presents with us. Hope you like them.

ADRIAN. Thanks. I'm sure I will.

MEG. And a cake, of course, I brought a cake. I didn't forget the cake. I'll just pop it in here. Won't be a moment. You've got milk in, have you, Adrian?

ADRIAN. Oh, yes. Plenty of milk.

MEG. Your Dad prefers a drop of milk...

(**MEG** *goes out to the kitchen.*)

MICKY. You're looking a bit washed out, lad. Been overdoing it, have you?

ADRIAN. No more than usual, no. Not been sleeping so well, that's all.

MEG. *(Offstage.)* What's this on the floor, then?

ADRIAN. *(Guiltily.)* What?

MEG. *(Offstage.)* Looks like a coat, a woman's coat.

(*She returns holding* **CHARITY**'s *coat.*)

Where did this come from?

MICKY. Hello, hello...

ADRIAN. Oh, that? Probably the cleaning woman's, I expect.

MEG. Oh. Smart cleaning woman, isn't she?

MICKY. With a coat like that? How much are you paying her?

(She drapes the coat over the sofa.)

MEG. I'll leave it here for now. Is that your vodka bottle in the sink, Adrian?

ADRIAN. Yes, a present from Uncle Hal.

MICKY. Lead you into bad ways, that one.

ADRIAN. I thought I'd have a drink, you know, seeing as it was my birthday.

MEG. Got through most of the bottle, by the look of it.

ADRIAN. Well, once you get going, you know.

MEG. Oh, I can't bear to think of it, sitting drinking all on your own on your birthday.

MICKY. *(Wagging a finger.)* Slippery slope! Slippery slope!

MEG. I have to say, you're looking peaky, love.

MICKY. I was just saying that. Been living it up, hasn't he? Secretly living it up, that's what I think. I bought you that book by the way, for your birthday.

ADRIAN. What book's that, Dad?

MICKY. "Fun with Figures". I know you're fond of figures in your line. You haven't already got it, have you?

ADRIAN. No, no. Sounds fun, thank you.

MEG. And I've brought you your usual. No surprise there.

ADRIAN. What's that, Mum?

MEG. New jumper. Smart new woolly jumper.

ADRIAN. Thank you.

MEG. Just finished it yesterday. I'll check the kettle.

(**MEG** *returns to the kitchenette.*)

ADRIAN. *(Stifling a yawn.)* How was the drive over, Dad? Alright, was it?

(Throughout the next, although struggling to stay awake, he begins to fall asleep.)

MICKY. Well, we started off alright. We got onto the A628, the Dodworth Road. Then, after the roundabout, we took the first exit onto the slip road, you know, where we met a bit of traffic, only minor, mark you, nothing serious. But once we got onto the M1 – we should never have done the M1, I should have known better – roadworks everywhere. Every two yards. Roadworks! Three solid miles of it. Nose to nose. Unbelievable. Then, when we finally did get off it onto the A610, there were more of them, roadworks at the A6130 at Radford, one lane closed completely, would you believe? Then onto the A6514, Western Boulevard, that's when we met the real hold-ups, then mercifully onto the A610, Nuthall Road. Fairly busy there too. Then, thank the Lord, onto the A6008 and the welcome sight of Maid Marion Way. Were we glad to see that? Then all we had left was to negotiate Canal Street. And you know what Canal...

(He tails off. **ADRIAN** *is gently snoring, now very fast asleep.)*

Adrian? Adrian, lad...?

(**MEG** *returns with a stand for the teapot together with a milk jug.*)

He's asleep. Lad's fallen fast asleep...

MEG. Oh, dear...

MICKY. He was asking about our journey. I were just telling him and he nodded off...

MEG. Not surprised. He would do, yes.

> *(Before she can put the things down on the coffee table, **CHARITY** enters from the bedroom. She is wearing **ADRIAN**'s sweater which creates the effect, on her at least, of being a very short minidress.)*

CHARITY. *(As she enters.)* Right, that's it! Times up! That's your two hours, darlin'. You had your two hours, I'm off!

MICKY. Who the hell are you?

MEG. Who are you?

> *(**ADRIAN** slumbers on, oblivious.)*

CHARITY. *(Seeing her coat.)* Oh, there it is, good! I'll have that. You might as well have this back, darlin'. Here!

> *(She peels off the sweater, tossing it onto the recumbent **ADRIAN**, momentarily revealing her state of undress beneath.)*

MICKY. Bloody hell fire!

MEG. *(Shocked.)* Who are you? Who is she? She can't be his cleaner, surely?

MICKY. I somehow doubt it.

CHARITY. *(Putting on her coat.)* Right! Bye-bye. I'm off.

> *(She moves to the front door.)*

MICKY. Hey! Hey! Hey! Excuse me! Just one moment, young woman! Where the hell do you think you're going? Are you what I think you are? Are you what I'm thinking you are?

CHARITY. *(Wheeling round, fiercely.)* Yes, most probably, I am. What about it? Wanna make something of it?

MICKY. Bloody hell!

MEG. I don't believe it, I don't believe it. Adrian would never stoop this low. Consorting with a woman like – someone like –

CHARITY. Someone like me, you mean? I'll tell you something about that one, your lovely son, shall I? When he wakes up, you give him a message from me. You can tell him, he's given me more fun, more pleasure, more sheer bloody satisfaction than the last thirty-five blokes I've had put together. He's special, him. You should be proud of him, you should. And once he comes out of his cupboard, he'll be even more special. You tell him, thank you from me. By rights, I should have paid him. Ta-ra, then.

>   (**CHARITY** *goes out, closing the front door. A stunned silence.* **ADRIAN** *snores on.*)

MEG. *(At last.)* Oh, Adrian, how could you?

>   (*She returns sorrowfully to the kitchen.*)

(As she goes.) How could he? How could he?

>   (**MICKY** *rises and crosses to* **ADRIAN**.)

MICKY. *(Softly, with pride.)* Well done, lad! Proud of you, son, right proud of you!

>   (*On this touching family tableau featuring a proud father and a recumbent son, there is a:*)

>   (*Blackout.*)

End of Act II Scene One

Scene Two

(Sonia's eighteenth. Thirty-eight years ago. Back in the family home, only now upstairs on the first floor in seventeen year old **ADRIAN**'s *bedroom. It is obsessively tidy with everything in its proper place, not a typical teenage boy's bedroom. A small divan bed, a desk with chair, an armchair, a small chest of drawers and a low bookshelf, filled mainly with mathematical textbooks, astronomy and astrophysics. On the desk, there are also some exercise and reference books indicative of interrupted homework. The room has one door leading to the landing. In the opposite corner a door to his clothes cupboard. There is also a window looking over the back garden. Currently, we are in the midst of* **ADRIAN**'s *sister Sonia's eighteenth birthday party, sounds of which can be heard both through the throb of insistent rock music through the floor and, outside in the garden through the closed window, the sounds of excited, lively female voices.* At the start,* **ADRIAN** *is sitting at his desk, currently staring at the door of his cupboard. There is knocking on the bedroom door.)*

MICKY. *(Off, calling through the door.)* Adrian! Are you in there? Mind if I come in, son?

*(**ADRIAN** swivels back so he now faces his desk, apparently in the midst of studying.)*

---

* A licence to produce BIRTHDAYS PAST, BIRTHDAYS PRESENT does not include a performance licence for any third-party or copyrighted music. Licensees should create an original composition or use music in the public domain. For further information, please see Music Use Note on page iii.

ADRIAN. Come in, Dad!

(**MICKY** *enters, now aged forty-two.*)

MICKY. Sorry to interrupt, lad. But your mum was wondering whether you're coming downstairs soon.

ADRIAN. Yes, I told her, Dad, I'll be done shortly. I just need to finish this first.

MICKY. What is it, then? Homework?

ADRIAN. It's this bloody calculus. It's doing my head in.

MICKY. Well, I can't help you there, son. When you were little just doing basics, you know, adding, subtracting, multiplying, I was fine with that. But you've left me well behind now. (*Staring over* **ADRIAN**'s *shoulder.*) Dear, oh dear, makes your eyes water just looking at it, doesn't it? Listen, your mum's fretting. Can you give it a rest, just for a moment, come down for five minutes? After all, it's your sister's birthday, lad.

ADRIAN. I know. I know it's her birthday. I'm sick of hearing about it. Going on all day, hasn't she?

MICKY. Well, it's an important one, isn't it? Her eighteenth. You should be down there for that, at least. I mean, I know you two, you don't get on all that well, do you, never have done. But I think you owe it to her to at least put in an appearance, lad.

ADRIAN. She doesn't want me down there. She's got all her friends, hasn't she? All her stuck-up university mates. (*Making posh noises.*) Oh, blah, blah, blahdy-dah!

MICKY. They're not all from her university, there's one or two local lasses, as well. You know, ones you're at school with, both of you.

ADRIAN. None I like very much. Besides, I'll be the only bloke down there, won't I? It's all women, isn't it? She's only invited her mates. I'll be the only bloke.

MICKY. Well, now! What are you complaining about? Take advantage of it while you can, eh?

ADRIAN. Joking.

MICKY. *(At the window.)* Just look at them all down there, tramping all over the flowerbeds. Half of them scarcely got any clothes on, either. It's freezing out there.

ADRIAN. *(With an anxious look towards the cupboard.)* Look, Dad, I do need to finish this, honestly. Could you just leave me a minute, please? Tell Mum, I'll be down presently. If I don't finish this, I'll be in dead trouble tomorrow.

MICKY. Right. Promise? I've got your promise, have I?

ADRIAN. Promise.

*(A particularly loud scream from below in the garden, draws **MICKY** back to the window.)*

MICKY. What the hell are they doing down there? Oh, no, they've got hold of your mother's gnome, now!

ADRIAN. Her what?

MICKY. Her gnome. They're playing silly-buggers with her gnome. They're all drunk as skunks, from the look of it. They're only on fruit punch, too. That's all we're allowing them. And that's diluted an' all. *(Rapping on the window and mouthing.)* Put that down! Put that back! No! Put it back! Else you'll break it! Yes, you! I'm talking to you, young lady!

*(**ADRIAN** continues to give anxious looks in the direction of the cupboard.)*

Women! They're alright on their own, most of them. Alright individually, but you're right, son, get them together like that, in a group, they're bloody lethal. Worse than the lads. I had a load of them in the coach, the other night, off for a hen night in Doncaster. I had to stop midway on the bypass. I said to them, girls, if you carry on behaving like that in my vehicle, it will constitute a danger to public safety and I'm dropping you off here and you can bloody walk the rest of the way!

ADRIAN. Dad! Do you mind, please?

MICKY. Alright. I'm going. I've got your promise on that? Five minutes.

ADRIAN. Five minutes.

(**MICKY** *goes out closing the door.*)

(*As soon as he's gone, calling.*) Okay, all clear! You can come out now!

(**HOPE**, *a plain, awkward girl of sixteen emerges. She is dressed in an unflattering party dress and clutches a small evening bag.*)

HOPE. It's suffocating in there. I got so hot, I could hardly breathe...

ADRIAN. Sorry. We don't have air conditioning, not in the cupboards.

HOPE. You've got a lot of shirts, haven't you? Lovely shirts and sweaters. Some really nice sweaters you've got, too. Did your mum knit them for you?

ADRIAN. Look, can you go now, please. What were you doing, anyway, rushing into the cupboard, like that? It was only my Dad. Why were you hiding from my Dad?

HOPE. He might have got wrong ideas, mightn't he?

ADRIAN. What if he had? It wasn't as if we were doing anything.

HOPE. We could have been, though, couldn't we?

ADRIAN. Well, we weren't.

HOPE. He wasn't to know, though, was he? He might have jumped to the wrong conclusion. Put two and two together, you know.

ADRIAN. In which case, he'd have made seven. What are you doing in here, anyway? I'm working. You just walked in without knocking...

HOPE. I told you, I was looking for the toilet. I needed the toilet. I got the wrong door, that's all.

ADRIAN. You didn't see the sign then, I take it?

HOPE. Sign?

ADRIAN. The sign on that door. It says, "Adrian only. Sisters not admitted."

HOPE. Oh, that.

ADRIAN. It could have been the toilet, I grant you. But that presupposes, doesn't it, that we have segregated toilets, my sister and me. Which I wish we did, but unfortunately we don't. The toilet's next door if you want it. Cheerio.

HOPE. *(Standing uncertainly.)* Actually. I didn't actually need the toilet. That were an excuse.

ADRIAN. Excuse for what?

HOPE. To see you. I wanted to see you.

ADRIAN. Why?

HOPE. I just – wanted to see you, that's all.

ADRIAN. You can see me at school. You see me practically every day at school, don't you?

HOPE. It's not the same at school, is it? Anyway, I don't always see you, not that often. You're the year above me. No, I wanted to see you here.

ADRIAN. Yes, well, now you've seen me, haven't you? So, bugger off, I'm working.

HOPE. Don't be like that!

ADRIAN. What?

HOPE. Don't be so unfriendly. You're so unfriendly, aren't you?

ADRIAN. Listen, I'm working. I need to concentrate on this. I'm sorry. But this happens to be my room and I'm busy. So, unless you have something important to say to me, would you kindly go away. Please!

(**HOPE** *continues to linger by the door.*)

Are you going or not? I warn you, I'll shove you out in a minute.

HOPE. Actually, the real reason I came up, the real reason was Sonia dared me.

ADRIAN. Sonia?

HOPE. Yes.

ADRIAN. I might have guessed my sister was behind it, I might have guessed. She dared you, you say? What exactly did she dare you to do?

HOPE. She dared me to – you know, come and talk to you.

ADRIAN. Yes, so? We've talked now, haven't we? You've won your dare. Well done. Congratulations. Off you go.

HOPE. *(Wriggling uncomfortably.)* No, it was more than that. She – dared me – to have – to have – you know… To have sex with you.

(*She now has his full attention.*)

ADRIAN. Sex? Did you say sex?

HOPE. Yes.

ADRIAN. With me? My sister dared you to have sex with me? Why?

HOPE. 'cos I'm the only one in our class that hasn't done it yet. The only one who hasn't had it.

ADRIAN. Oh, and you thought you might as well try me, did you?

HOPE. No...

ADRIAN. First bloke to hand. Oh, he'll do...

HOPE. No...

ADRIAN. Old Adrian, he'll do! Any port in a storm, eh?

HOPE. *(Distressed.)* No, it's not like that at all. Not at all. Sonia knows I'm – that I've got a thing for you, you know...

ADRIAN. *(Surprised.)* A thing for me?

HOPE. You must have noticed?

ADRIAN. No, I can't say I have.

HOPE. I've been giving you these looks, these special looks, for ages...

ADRIAN. How long has this been going on? How long have you had this thing for me?

HOPE. Years. I've been in love with you for years and years. Ever since I was eleven. Sonia knows that.

(A slight pause.)

Sorry. I thought you must have known. I thought you were just ignoring me. I thought you knew how I felt.

ADRIAN. *(Digesting this, softly.)* No, I had no idea. Christ! Since you were eleven, you say?

(She stands unhappily, jigging from one foot to the other.)

So? What did my brilliant sister suggest you did, when you came up here? What did she suggest?

HOPE. *(Unhappily.)* She told me to try and seduce you.

ADRIAN. *(Incredulously.)* Seduce me?

HOPE. You know, try and make you horny. She was a bit drunk, I think.

ADRIAN. I think you all are. Dad's fruit punch must be stronger than he thinks.

HOPE. No, we're not drinking that. No one's drinking that punch, it tastes of piss. We've brought in special supplies. Gin mostly. Bit of rum, you know.

ADRIAN. Who brought that in?

HOPE. I did.

ADRIAN. How did you get hold of it?

HOPE. I nicked it. My Dad runs the off-licence on the corner, doesn't he? That's the only reason I'm here. To supply the booze. The only reason Sonia invited me. She'd never have asked me otherwise.

> *(She is now tearful.)*

> *(**ADRIAN**'s attitude towards her noticeably softens.)*

ADRIAN. *(More gently.)* Sit down. *(Indicating the divan.)* Please, just sit down a minute.

> *(She sits on the edge of the divan, a little self-consciously.)*

(Picking his words carefully.) Listen, Hope, love. Sonia's – my sister's – she's alright, you know, but just occasionally she can be quite a – quite a cruel person, you know. Not bad exactly, I don't think she means to be cruel. Probably not even aware of it half the time. But she's a strong person, you know, very ambitious. She usually gets what she wants. She tends to use people a bit. People who generally aren't quite so strong

as she is. I know that because I grew up with her. She made my life that miserable sometimes, I can tell you. *(Smiling.)* Practically put me off women for life, she did. I think what she's doing in this case, Hope, she's just taking advantage of you, you know. Of the feelings you have for me. Maybe she thinks of it as a bit of a laugh...

HOPE. A laugh?

ADRIAN. She was just setting you up, love. Sending you up here. Telling you to try and seduce me. It's her idea of a joke, that's all. Sorry. I'm sorry. She shouldn't have done that to you.

> *(He places his hand gently on hers and they connect for the very first time.)*

HOPE. You're not, are you?

ADRIAN. I'm not what?

HOPE. Feeling horny? You're not feeling horny at all, are you?

ADRIAN. No. Not in the least horny. Sorry.

HOPE. Well, I'd better go, hadn't I?

> *(Her last ray of hope dashed, she moves sadly to the door.)*

ADRIAN. *(Coming to a decision.)* Listen, I don't think we should let her get away with this, you know, I really don't.

HOPE. *(Turning, startled.)* How do you mean?

ADRIAN. *(Rising, as he gets angrier.)* Why should she get away with it, eh? Why the hell should she get away with it again? Making a fool of you? Making fools of us both, in a way? No, I'm sick of her! I'm sick of her always bloody doing this, manipulating people, for her own... Look, we'll say we've done it, shall we? We'll tell her you did seduce me. I got incredibly horny and then we had it away – gloriously had it away – on that bed. No, better still, in that cupboard,

HOPE. In the cupboard? Why in the cupboard?

ADRIAN. More convincing. More spontaneous. More spur of the moment. If we made love out here, they'd hear your screams of pleasure, wouldn't they? No, you seduced me and I grabbed hold of you by your hair –

HOPE. No, not by my hair, please –

ADRIAN. – by the scruff of your neck, then, and I dragged you into that cupboard to muffle the sound, threw you to the floor, pinned you down helplessly whimpering and we made violent passionate love in amongst my hand knitted sweaters! How's that sound?

HOPE. *(Getting excited.)* Oh, sounds wonderful...

ADRIAN. Are you right? You right with that, are you? That do you?

HOPE. *(Her eyes aglow.)* Oh, yes, yes, yes!

> *(They stand facing each other, both slightly breathless.)*

ADRIAN. We're not really going to do that, though.

HOPE. We're not?

ADRIAN. No, that's what we're going to tell them we did.

HOPE. What are we actually going to do, then?

ADRIAN. What we are actually going to do is you are going back downstairs while I finish my calculus revision in order that I can achieve my lifetime ambition and become an astrophysicist. But we tell them that's what happened. That's what we tell them.

HOPE. Tell who?

ADRIAN. Whoever you want. Your classmates. Sonia. Especially bloody Sonia.

HOPE. But they'll never believe me, will they? They'll know I'm making it up.

ADRIAN. Not if I back you up, they won't. And I will, I'll back you up, don't worry. Just to see the look of amazement on my sister's stupid face. Realising her nasty little joke had backfired. Our word against theirs, isn't it?

    (**HOPE** *considers for a moment.*)

HOPE. You'll back me up, then? You won't suddenly turn round and tell people it isn't true?

ADRIAN. I won't, if you don't.

HOPE. Swear?

ADRIAN. I swear

HOPE. Till your dying day?

ADRIAN. Till my dying day.

HOPE. *(Proffering her lips.)* Seal it with a kiss, then.

ADRIAN. With a kiss.

    (*They kiss. For probably longer than strictly necessary but still well short of what she had hoped for.*)

HOPE. That was wonderful! Was it good for you?

ADRIAN. Yes. It was good for me.

HOPE. *(Hopefully.)* You're sure you're not feeling a little bit...?

ADRIAN. Better stick to plan A, hadn't we?

HOPE. *(Rather sadly.)* I suppose.

ADRIAN. *(Moving to the cupboard.)* I'd better create a bit of mayhem in here. Back up the story... Just a second.

> *(He goes into the cupboard.)*

> *(She opens her bag and consults her hand mirror.)*

HOPE. *(Studying herself.)* Better make it look as if I'd just had it, too.

> *(She messes up her hair a bit.)*

> *(From the window another wild shriek of girlish mirth in the garden.)*

> *(She moves to look out. Impulsively, she opens the window.)*

(Calling.) Sonia! Sonia! Sonzee!

> *(She punches the air in triumph.)*

(Calling.) What you mean, he's boring? He's gorgeous! He's totally gorgeous! Hey, girl, what's more you owe me five quid!

> *(She closes the window.)*

> *(**ADRIAN** returns.)*

ADRIAN. What are you doing?

HOPE. *(Elatedly punching the air again.)* Yeah!

> *(She moves to the door.)*

(Turning.) Promise, now? You won't tell? Swear on your life?

ADRIAN. On my life.

> *(She goes out, closing the door.)*

(**ADRIAN** *stands for a moment.*)

(*Shaking his head.*) I've never understood women. Doubt I ever will, either.

> (*As he sits down again at his desk to resume his homework, there is a loud cheer from the garden outside. Curious, he stands and looks out. The sounds continue. He opens the window and there is an especially loud cheer and applause from the twenty or so young women gathered below. He acknowledges this with embarrassed bewilderment. He shakes his head in complete mystification, a feeling which, as regards the opposite sex, will remain with him for the rest of his life. As he stands bemused and the applause and cheering continues, the lights fade to:*)

(*Blackout.*)

End of Play

ABOUT THE AUTHOR

Alan Ayckbourn has worked in theatre as a playwright and director for over fifty years, rarely if ever tempted by television or film, which perhaps explains why he continues to be so prolific. To date he has written more than eighty plays, many one-act plays and a large amount of work for the younger audience. His work has been translated into over thirty-five languages, is performed on stage and television throughout the world and has won countless awards.

Major successes include: *Relatively Speaking, How the Other Half Loves, Absurd Person Singular, Bedroom Farce, A Chorus of Disapproval,* and *The Norman Conquests.* In recent years, there have been revivals of *Season's Greetings* and *A Small Family Business* at the National Theatre; in the West End *Absent Friends, A Chorus of Disapproval, Relatively Speaking* and *How the Other Half Loves*; and at Chichester Festival Theatre, major revivals of *Way Upstream* in 2015 and *The Norman Conquests* in 2017. 2019 also saw the publication of his first work of prose fiction, *The Divide.*

Artistic director of the Stephen Joseph Theatre from 1972–2009, where almost all his plays have been first staged, he continues to direct his latest new work there. He was honoured to be appointed the SJT's first Director Emeritus during 2018. He has been inducted into the American Theater Hall of Fame, received the 2010 Critics' Circle Award for Services to the Arts and became the first British playwright to receive both Olivier and Tony Special Lifetime Achievement Awards. He was knighted in 1997 for services to the theatre.

Other plays by ALAN AYCKBOURN
published and licensed by Concord Theatricals

Absent Friends

Arrivals and Departures

Awaking Beauty

Bedroom Farce

Better Off Dead

Body Language

A Brief History of Women

Callisto 5

The Champion of Paribanou

A Chorus of Disapproval

Comic Potential

Communicating Doors

Confusions

Consuming Passions

A Cut in the Rates

Dreams from a Summer House

Drowning on Dry Land

Ernie's Incredible Illucinations

Family Circles

Farcicals

FlatSpin

GamePlan

Gizmo

Haunting Julia

Henceforward...

Hero's Welcome

House & Garden

How the Other Half Loves

If I Were You

Improbable Fiction

Intimate Exchanges, Volume I

Intimate Exchanges, Volume II

It Could Be Any One of Us

Joking Apart

Just Between Ourselves

Life and Beth

Life of Riley

Living Together

Man of the Moment

Me, Myself and I

Mixed Doubles

Mr A's Amazing Maze Plays

Mr Whatnot

My Very Own Story

My Wonderful Day

Neighbourhood Watch

No Knowing

The Norman Conquests: Table Manners; Living Together; Round and Round the Garden

Private Fears in Public Places

Relatively Speaking

The Revengers' Comedies

RolePlay

Roundelay

Season's Greetings

Sisterly Feelings

A Small Family Business

Snake in the Grass

Suburban Strains

Sugar Daddies

Taking Steps

Ten Times Table

Things We Do for Love

This Is Where We Came In

Time and Time Again

Time of My Life

Tons of Money (revised)

Way Upstream

Wildest Dreams

Wolf at the Door

Woman in Mind

A Word from Our Sponsor

**Other plays by ALAN AYCKBOURN
licensed by Concord Theatricals**

The Boy Who Fell Into a Book

Invisible Friends

The Jollies

Orvin – Champion of Champions

Surprises

Whenever

Lightning Source UK Ltd.
Milton Keynes UK
UKHW011605160421
382087UK00009B/558